D1378378

# The Attack
# on Pearl
# Harbor

PERSPECTIVES ON

# The Attack on Pearl Harbor

## U.S. Entry into World War II

## MICHAEL BURGAN

Marshall Cavendish
Benchmark
New York

Copyright © 2012 Marshall Cavendish Corporation

Published by Marshall Cavendish Benchmark
An imprint of Marshall Cavendish Corporation

All rights reserved.

No part of this publication may be reproduced, stored in a retrieval system or transmitted, in any form or by any means, electronic, mechanical, photocopying, recording, or otherwise, without the prior permission of the copyright owner. Request for permission should be addressed to the Publisher, Marshall Cavendish Corporation, 99 White Plains Road, Tarrytown, NY 10591. Tel: (914) 332-8888, fax: (914) 332-1888.
Website: www.marshallcavendish.us

This publication represents the opinions and views of the author based on Michael Burgan's personal experience, knowledge, and research. The information in this book serves as a general guide only. The author and publisher have used their best efforts in preparing this book and disclaim liability rising directly and indirectly from the use and application of this book.

Other Marshall Cavendish Offices:
Marshall Cavendish International (Asia) Private Limited, 1 New Industrial Road, Singapore 536196
• Marshall Cavendish International (Thailand) Co Ltd. 253 Asoke, 12th Flr, Sukhumvit 21 Road, Klongtoey Nua, Wattana, Bangkok 10110, Thailand • Marshall Cavendish (Malaysia) Sdn Bhd, Times Subang, Lot 46, Subang Hi-Tech Industrial Park, Batu Tiga, 40000 Shah Alam, Selangor Darul Ehsan, Malaysia

Marshall Cavendish is a trademark of Times Publishing Limited

All websites were available and accurate when this book was sent to press.

Library of Congress Cataloging-in-Publication Data
Burgan, Michael.
The attack on Pearl Harbor : U.S. entry into World War II / Michael Burgan.
p. cm. — (Perspectives on)
Includes bibliographical references and index.
Summary: "Provides comprehensive information on the bombing of Pearl Harbor in 1941 and the differing perspectives accompanying it"—Provided by publisher.
ISBN 978-1-60870-448-4 (print)   978-0-60870-720-1 (ebook)

1. Pearl Harbor (Hawaii), Attack on, 1941—Juvenile literature. 2. World War, 1939–1945—Causes—Juvenile literature. 3. United States—Foreign relations—Japan—Juvenile literature. 4. Japan—Foreign relations—United States—Juvenile literature. I. Title.
D767.92.B76 2012
940.54´26693—dc22
2010030334

Editor: Christine Florie
Publisher: Michelle Bisson
Art Director: Anahid Hamparian
Series Designer: Sonia Chaghatzbanian

Expert Reader: Cathal J. Nolan, associate professor of history, executive director International History Institute, Boston University, Boston, Massachusetts

Photo research by Marybeth Kavanagh

Cover photo by US Navy/Time Life Pictures/Getty Images

The photographs in this book are used by permission and through the courtesy of: *SuperStock*: 2-3; Everett Collection, 15; Stock Connection, 105; *Naval Historical Foundation*: 8, 59, 68; *Getty Images*: Hulton Archive, 11; Roger Viollet, 46; MPI, 90; *AP Photo*: 19, 44, 62, 71; HWG, 93; Kyodo, 106; *Corbis*: Bettmann, 25; *The Granger Collection, New York*: 27, 32, 37; *The Image Works*: Ullstein bild, 47; akg-images, 76; *Alamy*: Buddy Mays, 107

Printed in Malaysia (T)
1 3 5 6 4 2

# Contents

# Introduction

MORE THAN TWO THOUSAND years ago, Chinese generals read these famous words: "All warfare is based on deception . . . when we are near, we must make the enemy believe we are far away." Ancient ideas about secrecy and deception have remained a part of military tactics, as one of the key events of the twentieth century shows.

On December 7, 1941, Japan executed one of the most remarkable examples of military deception in world history. U.S. military commanders at Pearl Harbor, Hawaii, were caught off guard when Japanese naval and air forces attacked.

For Japan and the United States, some perspectives on Pearl Harbor are easy to see. For the Japanese, Pearl Harbor seemed to be a military necessity, to continue their leaders' plan of conquest in Asia. Although U.S. leaders had expected war to break out with Japan, they were surprised by the site of the attack. The U.S. population saw the attack as the height of treachery and felt deceived by Japanese actions and words that had preceded it. After being so badly caught off guard, Americans wanted to know how such a surprise attack could have gone undetected until the very last minute, and they sought to lay blame on specific individuals. The attack on Pearl Harbor also fueled racist attitudes toward the Japanese that had been building for decades, as well as racist attitudes toward Americans on the part of the Japanese.

But there were other perspectives in the months leading up to Pearl Harbor and in the decades that followed. Not all Japanese leaders wanted a war with the United States. They knew the Americans could outspend and outbuild them militarily: winning the battle at Pearl Harbor could still mean losing the war. And after the event, some Americans saw the devastating losses at Pearl Harbor as avoidable. Without any evidence to support their belief, a few even believed that President Franklin D. Roosevelt had welcomed the attack as a way to enter World War II, which had been raging in Europe since 1939. Roosevelt's critics claimed that the president and others lied or covered up facts to keep the truth of Pearl Harbor hidden. Backers of Roosevelt, and all available evidence assembled by historians, support the position that the president did not sacrifice U.S. ships and citizens to bring the country into the war via a "back door." Human error and misunderstandings played a large part in the failure to foresee the attack on Pearl Harbor.

With so many perspectives and historical angles, the attack on Pearl Harbor has fascinated many people, scholars and average citizens alike. Even though historians agree that the research done over the decades has conclusively answered the original questions that surrounded the tactical success of the Japanese surprise attack, in popular memory some of the controversy remains.

# One

# A Deadly Sunday Morning

HIGH ABOVE A THICK LAYER of clouds, Japanese commander Mitsuo Fuchida flew in his warplane. More than 10,000 feet below him, stiff winds stirred the waters of the Pacific Ocean. Over the water and the clouds, 182 more Japanese aircraft shared the skies with Fuchida. Some carried bombs, while others had torpedoes. Protecting them from possible enemy planes were Japanese Zero fighters, among the best planes in the world.

As Fuchida flew on, cracks in the clouds let him see his flight's destination: the Hawaiian island of Oahu, home of the U.S. naval fleet based at Pearl Harbor. Peering through binoculars, Fuchida saw the ships lined up at their docks. He told his radio operator to signal the other planes: "TO, TO, TO." "TO" stood for *totsugeki*, the Japanese word for "charge." The attack was on. Soon Fuchida sent a second message: "TORA, TORA, TORA." This repetition of the Japanese word for "tiger" meant that Fuchida and his pilots had achieved complete tactical surprise: there were no American fighters waiting to defend the ships, and no anti-aircraft fire rising to greet the Japanese planes.

Japanese naval aircraft prepare to take off from an aircraft carrier to attack Pearl Harbor during the morning of December 7, 1941.

## Missed Chances

Fuchida didn't know, however, that some of his planes had been detected. That Sunday morning of December 7, 1941, U.S. Army privates George Elliott and Joseph Lockard were stationed at one of Oahu's early-warning radar systems. They both saw something on their radar screen. Lockard later called it "the biggest sighting he had ever seen"—some fifty or so planes, about 130 miles away. The two enlisted men thought their equipment might be broken, but tests revealed no malfunctions. They debated sending a message to the Information Center, where officers were stationed. Finally they called, and a young lieutenant told them to ignore the sighting. Some B-17 bombers were due to reach Hawaii from the West Coast, the junior officer explained. The blips on the radar screen were probably those planes. But in reporting to the center, Lockard had failed to state how many planes the radar had revealed. The fifty he and Elliott detected were more than three times the number of friendly B-17s due in from California. Lockard might not have been told, "Don't worry about it" if the Information Center had known what the privates had really seen—the first wave of a Japanese strike force heading to bomb Hawaii's airfields and the great battleships lined up in Pearl Harbor.

The radar sighting of the Japanese planes was not even the first sign that something was wrong on the American side that Sunday morning. Before 7 a.m., when Fuchida's planes were still beyond radar range, U.S. ships had detected several Japanese minisubmarines. Five of the tiny subs, carrying two torpedoes each, had been launched from much larger underwater vessels that remained out at sea. Around 6:45, a U.S. destroyer sank one of the minisubs close to the harbor, but word of the attack was not fully credited by the navy and never reached the army at all. The army, not the navy, had the ultimate duty of protecting the U.S. ships in dock and the rest of Oahu. Around 7:30 word of the attack reached Admiral Husband E. Kimmel, commander of the U.S. fleet at Pearl Harbor. He wanted to check the reports himself, since in the preceding weeks he had received false reports about enemy subs in the waters off Oahu. As time slipped by, Fuchida's 183 planes neared their unsuspecting targets.

## The Assault on Pearl Harbor

Just before 8 a.m., the Japanese dropped their first bombs on several airfields on Oahu, aiming for U.S. warplanes on

A photograph taken from a Japanese bomber shows a burning Wheeler Airfield after their attack.

# Hawaii, the United States, and the Japanese

Japanese people began arriving on the Hawaiian islands to work during the 1860s. Most took jobs on large sugarcane and pineapple plantations. Hawaii was an independent kingdom then, but Americans already had a presence as Christian missionaries. U.S. companies also invested in the islands' plantations and other businesses. The United States took control of Hawaii in 1898 and made it a U.S. territory two years later. The Japanese continued to play an important role in Hawaii's economy, and by 1923 they were the single largest ethnic group there. In the months before the Pearl Harbor attack, the presence of so many Japanese Americans made it easy for Japanese spies to move freely about the island. Their numbers also made U.S. officials fearful of sabotage by Japanese Americans loyal to Japan. Still, a government report prepared before the attack said that during a possible war with Japan, "we believe the big majority . . . would be neutral or even actively loyal" to the United States. That report, however, did not end the fears of some Americans after Pearl Harbor, when anger over the attack sparked deep suspicion of many innocent Japanese.

the ground. Some Americans, barely out of bed, heard the noise and thought the navy was conducting drills. But a few quickly realized that Pearl Harbor was under attack. A radio report confirmed it: "This is no test. Pearl Harbor is being bombed by the Japanese!"

As the bombs fell on the airfields, the Japanese bombers flew low over the harbor, releasing their explosives and torpedoes. The U.S. Navy had about one hundred ships in port that morning, but the Japanese concentrated on the largest, the battleships and cruisers. The torpedoes cut through the shallow water of Pearl Harbor, striking the U.S. ships below the surface. Meanwhile, bombers high above also released their loads. Many bombs hit the battleship USS *Arizona*, but one was the deadliest. It reached the magazine, the armored room deep inside the ship where ammunition was stored, and set off a massive blast. More than one thousand sailors lost their lives, either killed by the bombs or drowned in the harbor trapped inside the ship. Nearby, other battleships took crippling hits.

As the explosions ripped through the morning's quiet, the sky began to fill with black smoke. Above it, the Japanese Zeros shot down some of the handful of U.S. planes that escaped the bombing and managed to get off the ground. Then the enemy began firing at the Americans scrambling for antiaircraft guns both on land and aboard the ships. Some of the defenders reached their guns and fired at the attackers, but still the Japanese planes roared over the harbor.

The attack lasted until about 8:30 a.m. As the last Japanese planes flew out of view, soldiers, sailors, and marines prepared for a new round of attacks. The Japanese did soon return, as a second wave of planes aimed for ships that had

The USS *West Virginia* burns in the bombing of Pearl Harbor.

mostly escaped damage before. This time, the American gunners had more success against the Japanese, shooting down twenty-nine planes. Still, when the second and last attack ended, the signs of a Japanese victory were clear. Bombs and torpedoes had sunk or damaged twenty-one ships, and more than three hundred U.S. warplanes were destroyed, mostly on the ground. The dead totaled more than 2,400 Americans, while another 1,178 were wounded.

## The Americans React

Details of the attack, which had begun around 1:30 p.m. Eastern Standard Time, started reaching President Franklin D. Roosevelt in the White House within an hour. The president's

# Attacker, Defender

For Japanese sailors and airmen, the attack on Pearl Harbor had been preceded by months of training and preparation, ending in several hours of precise action. For the Americans on land or on ships, the attack was a complete surprise. Here are two views of several moments during the attack.

Mitsuo Fuchida, commander of the Japanese planes:

> I . . . lay flat on the cockpit floor and slid open a peephole cover in order to observe the fall of the bombs. I watched four bombs plummet. The target—two battleships moored side by side—lay ahead. The bombs became smaller and smaller and finally disappeared. I held my breath until two tiny puffs of smoke flashed suddenly on the ship to the left, and I shouted, "Two hits!"

Louis Mathieson, sailor on the USS *Oklahoma*:

*We were just about to enter the shower when the general alarm went off. . . . Just then, BOOM! The ship seemed to dip forward a little. Actually, the bow came up. . . . Then we were hit by another torpedo . . . the ship seemed to leap up about a foot and a half, or maybe just the deck under me. The noise was horrendous. There were two explosions. I can recall seven torpedo hits in all. . . . Some of these hits were simultaneous. With the second hit, my feet were knocked out from under me, and I landed on the deck. . . . I thought I was going to die at any moment.*

secretary, Grace Tully, remembered that "each report [was] more terrible than the last," and each left Roosevelt shaking his head. Still, as more news came in, Roosevelt seemed calm. For months, he and his advisers had been talking with Japan, trying to avoid a war, while also preparing to accept war if negotiations failed. Roosevelt was almost certain that war would come as Japan's government pursued an increasingly reckless and aggressive policy of war in China and made threats toward smaller nations in Southeast Asia. Roosevelt did not want to strike the first blow, but he was ready to accept war if Japan, which had invaded China in 1937, would not cease its brutal aggression there.

For just over two years, Roosevelt had tried to help the British and their allies against Germany, short of going to war. Sometimes he acted publicly, working with Congress. Also, however, he secretly ordered military actions that supported Britain but risked direct conflict with Germany, which in turn might bring the United States into the European war. With the Pearl Harbor attack, aide Harry Hopkins said, "the Japanese had made the decision for him" about going to war with Japan. And now, as they digested the news of a surprise attack that had killed more than 2,400 of their fellow citizens, Americans rallied around the president and the war effort.

The next day, Roosevelt went before Congress, asking the legislature to acknowledge that a state of war existed with the empire of Japan. He called December 7, 1941, "a date which will live in infamy" as "the United States of America was suddenly and deliberately attacked by . . . the empire of Japan." Congress quickly voted for war against Japan. Italy and Germany, Japan's allies, then declared war on the

On December 8, 1941, one day after the attack on Pearl Harbor, President Franklin Delano Roosevelt appeared before a joint session of Congress asking for an immediate declaration of war.

United States. They believed that the Japanese Navy would tie down the Americans in the Pacific, preventing U.S. forces from playing a major role in Europe. World War II had entered a new phase.

# Two

# First Step toward War

Oahu, Hawaii, is a place of sandy beaches and pleasant tropical temperatures. Tourists have come there to relax for more than a century. What attracted the U.S. Navy to the site was Oahu's large natural port—the perfect spot for docking ships. Still, before 1940, Pearl Harbor was not a major naval base. The port was home to one aircraft carrier and its support ships. Warships based on the West Coast sometimes stopped there. But as tensions rose with Japan during 1939 and 1940, the United States made Pearl Harbor the center of its Pacific defenses.

The roots of the increasingly stormy relationship went back several decades. In the years before Pearl Harbor, Japan and the United States had emerged as two major players in the Pacific region. Neither wanted to see the other dominate trade or gain military superiority. Greater military strength would give one country the ability to restrict the goals of the other in the region. But as each country became stronger, it also tried to use diplomacy to keep peaceful relations, even as some leaders, particularly in Japan, sensed that conflict would someday be likely.

## Sea Power

In an era when airplanes and rockets did not exist, a powerful navy was essential for a nation to build its overseas trade. Merchant ships carried the goods, while naval vessels made sure that the merchant fleet remained safe at sea and had access to foreign ports. Both the Americans and the Japanese valued a strong navy to protect their respective interests in the Pacific.

By the end of the nineteenth century, the Americans were particularly interested in trading with China. They called for an "open door" policy that encouraged free trade between the Chinese and Americans, without any interference from other nations active in China. Japan, though, would become a growing concern, as it increased its influence in China.

During World War I, the United States and Japan fought on the same side against Germany. During the war, Japan expanded its influence in China, a failing state torn by civil wars and dominated by warlords. In addition, Japan had already gained control of some mainland territory over the objections of the Chinese. The United States and other nations opposed Japan's efforts to make further inroads into China and were wary of its role as an increasingly influential international force.

Japan presented a threat to the U.S. Open Door policy. Japan wanted to end China's trade with other nations so that Japan could have the market for itself. The Americans wanted an "open door" in China, and this would require free trade between the two countries, without foreign interference. In contrast, Japan wanted to monopolize that trade, which it would accomplish by closing the door to external trade with China. In the years to come, China would be at the center of U.S.–Japanese diplomatic disputes.

After World War I, some younger members of Japan's military welcomed their country's growing influence and were angered by a decision the national government made in 1922. In that year, at the Washington Naval Conference, Japan and other nations with large navies had agreed to limits on the number of large warships each country could build. World leaders hoped to reduce the risk of future world wars. The limits forced three great naval powers—Great Britain, the United States, and Japan—to dismantle some existing ships.

Japan's younger military leaders, who wanted free rein to continue developing their country's navy, opposed the limits set down at the conference. Older military and civilian leaders, however, generally favored peaceful relations with other world powers and thought the results of the Washington conference promoted those goals. A split between military and governmental factions was set in motion, and it would continue to grow.

During the first years of the twentieth century, as its military expanded, Japan had created the Imperial National Defense Policy—its secret blueprint for military affairs and national security. After the Washington conference, some of the younger officers helped shape a new version of the policy that took written form in 1923. The document stated that the United States was the most likely enemy in any future major war and pointed out that Japanese control of China would be threatened by the U.S. desire for trade with the huge, undeveloped country. The policy also noted the racist attitudes many Americans along the Pacific Coast displayed toward the Japanese. No mention, however, was made of the feeling by many of their own nationals that the Japanese were more "racially pure" than other Asians. The policy cited growing U.S. military power in the Pacific, thanks partly to its bases in the Philippines and Hawaii, and concluded that a "clash with our Empire will become inevitable sooner or later. In short, the Imperial National Defense Policy must be primarily directed against the United States."

More conferences on naval power followed. One held in London in 1930 left the more militaristic Japanese naval officers angry because their government had agreed to limits on the Japanese Navy greater than the one placed on U.S. forces. One Japanese critic said the agreement was as if Japan had been "bound hand and foot and thrown into jail" by the British and Americans. In both the government and the military, nationalists seeking a stronger Japan continued to argue with more moderate forces; but the militarists were increasingly winning the day—sometimes by means of assassinating their enemies in the military and the civilian government.

## To Isolate, or Not

The 1930s saw a continuing argument over policy in the United States as well. Since the end of World War I, the country had been divided over how to pursue its foreign policy. Some thought the United States should take an active role in world affairs. These Americans were known as interventionists or internationalists. Those who opposed this active role, called isolationists or noninterventionists, particularly wanted the United States to stay out of foreign wars unless the country were directly attacked. Isolationist feelings only increased as the country struggled with the economic problems created by

# Anti-Japanese Feelings

In the early twentieth century, growing American racism toward Japanese immigrants sometimes strained relations between the United States and Japan. Some West Coast states restricted Japanese Americans' access to schools and denied to some the right to own land. Finally, the anti-Japanese feelings led to the almost total elimination of Japanese immigration to the United States. In 1922, in *Ozawa v. United States*, the U.S. Supreme Court ruled that Asians could not become naturalized citizens. The Court cited a 1906 law that permitted naturalization for whites or people of African descent only. Two years later, Congress used the *Ozawa* ruling to restrict all emigrants from Japan. The 1924 Immigration Act said that people who could not become naturalized Americans, such as the Japanese, could not enter the country at all. The Japanese ambassador to the United States resigned in protest of the 1924 act,

coming as it did after years of anti-Japanese laws. In Japan, several anti-American riots broke out, reflecting a general anger against the U.S. law and the deeper attitude of racism it reflected.

the Great Depression, which began in 1929 and lasted right up to the start of World War II. Most Americans wanted to focus on their own problems and not get tangled in overseas events.

That isolationist majority remained in place even after Japan used military force in China to expand its control there. In 1931 Japan invaded a region to the north of China called Manchuria and soon set up a puppet government whose leaders were more loyal to Japanese Army officers in the territory than to leaders in Tokyo. The Japanese falsely claimed the military action was self-defense, to protect its interest there. Hirosi Saito, a Japanese diplomat in the United States, said Japan "has no territorial ambitions" in Manchuria and thought the military clash "is after all nothing but a passing storm."

But in reality, the aggressive military thrust reflected the belief among nearly all leading Japanese military and civilian officials by 1931 that their country needed to seize natural resources from other parts of Asia to keep its industry growing and to maintain Japan's status as a world power. The country also needed land to accommodate its rising population. And some Japanese thought they had a natural right to dominate supposedly weaker and inferior peoples in Asia. The Japanese had a duty, in this thinking, to lead Asia in a great battle against the West, and specifically the United States. That thinking, though, was just cover for Japan's own imperialist designs on the countries in its own neighborhood.

## A Quiet Response

Japan's actions angered U.S. leaders, but they were not ready to go to war with Japan over the Manchurian invasion.

This American cartoon was created in 1931 and comments on Japan's seizure of Manchuria and its failure to keep promises and international treaty agreements.

Neither was anyone else, not even the Chinese. The U.S. government instead called for the preservation of its trade rights in China and refused to recognize the pro-Japanese government in Manchuria. Japan reacted to international criticism by condemning it and walking out of the League of Nations, forerunner to the United Nations.

When Franklin Roosevelt took over the presidency in 1933, he showed the same restraint with Japan as President

Herbert Hoover had before him. Roosevelt was focused on easing the devastating effects of the Great Depression, which had thrown millions of Americans out of work. Still, Roosevelt, more so than the three Republican presidents who had preceded him, was an internationalist. He saw how the fate of the United States was tied to events around the world. But as assistant secretary of the navy during World War I, he knew of the horrors of combat. Keeping the peace around the world was a major goal.

Roosevelt was also a skilled politician. He knew that if he wanted continued support from voters and from lawmakers in Congress, he had to pay attention to their wishes. He had to respect the general isolationist attitude held by many Americans. In foreign affairs, Roosevelt spent most of the late 1930s balancing his desire to keep the support of isolationists while drawing the country's attention to growing international dangers.

Roosevelt didn't like the Japanese presence in Manchuria, but he wasn't ready to take action there. And for the Japanese, nothing short of war would make them give up their gains. Konoe Fumimaro, a rising figure in Japan's government, later wrote that "Japan's action in Manchuria is indispensable for Japan's existence." To preserve its economic strength, the nation had to expand in Asia and weaken the influence of Western countries. Those desires set the Japanese on the path to invasions of a dozen countries, and to war on multiple fronts after the attack on Pearl Harbor.

# Three
# Rising Tensions Across the Pacific

AFTER INVADING MANCHURIA in 1931, Japan increased its control over parts of China, and the military increased its influence over the government. Japan was swept by a growing wave of nationalism, the belief that Japan was destined for greatness. Ienaga Saburō, a teacher in Japan, noted later that "ordinary Japanese citizens were taught from schoolbooks compiled by the state, and were made to believe that Japan was a superior nation whose mission was to lead the world . . . the citizenry as a whole accepted these things as the truth." More young military officers wanted both to assert Japan's greatness and to continue to weaken Western influence in Asia. To the people at large, the militarists offered the hope of ending the influence of Japan's wealthy elite, who seemed to only pursue their own interests.

During a military rebellion in 1936, the rebels expressed a clear anti-elitist view. As they attacked leading government officials, they released a statement to the press. "In recent years . . . there have appeared many persons whose chief aim and purpose have been to amass personal material wealth, disregarding the general welfare and prosperity of the Japanese people." The rebels were defeated and their leaders executed. But the military ended up with greater control over the cabinet, the emperor's top advisers. They would begin to pursue a more militaristic, openly aggressive strategy.

In early 1937 the military's desire to expand farther into China was not shared by some civilian leaders. Konoe Fumimaro had become Japan's prime minister after the failed rebellion. Fumimaro thought Japan was not strong enough to wage a major war, and he feared a Western response to further Japanese aggression in China. Still, the prime minister went along with the military's request to send more troops to Manchuria. The Japanese people welcomed this show of strength; the Chinese, not surprisingly, opposed it. Soon, a full-scale war had erupted in provinces outside Manchuria.

Franklin Roosevelt denounced Japan's advance through China. Nationalist Japanese leaders rejected any criticism. Diplomat Yosuke Matsuoka claimed that Japan was not seeking new wealth for its own sake: "No treasure trove is in [Japan's] eyes—only sacrifices upon sacrifices. . . . But her very life depends on it, as do those of her neighbors as well." Japan always explained its advances as extending a helping hand to fellow Asians. The Japanese would drive out European colonial rulers so the Dutch East Indies and other regions could develop their resources for themselves, rather than sending them to Europe. But in reality, Japan wanted the resources for itself, and its rule in conquered lands was far more harsh during the war than any European rule over Asian colonies, except for the Dutch in Indochina.

In China, the Japanese army continued its war. In July 1939, aiming to cut off Japan's access to supplies critical to its war effort, Roosevelt declared that the United States would end an old trade agreement with Japan. However, Japan was prepared to fight on in China. And some Japanese

# The Marco Polo Bridge

Near Beijing, China, a simple incident at a bridge named after a famous Westerner helped spark the growth of war in Asia. On July 7, 1937, Japanese troops stationed in China exchanged shots with Chinese soldiers near the Marco Polo Bridge. No one knows who fired the first shot, and local officials soon reached a truce that seemed to end the matter. But the militarists in Japan used the incident as their excuse to invade northern China. The bloody war Japan then waged in China convinced Franklin Roosevelt that Japan was a growing threat to world peace. The Americans indirectly and in a minor way supported the Chinese in their war with Japan, while Japan moved much closer to alliance with the fascist aggressors in Europe. U.S.–Japanese relations began to weaken, setting the two countries on the path to Pearl Harbor.

This cartoon by D. R. Fitzpatrick, entitled "Piece by Piece," shows Japan's expansionism in Asia.

military leaders were increasingly preparing for a possible war with the United States.

By this time, the major antiwar arguments no longer

existed within the Japanese government. Military success in China and a small share of the wealth generated in newly conquered lands led to greater popular support for nationalist policies. The fervor for more foreign military conquest led the Diet, Japan's nominal lawmaking body, to turn over control of the country to the military. After 1938 the military-dominated government could force individuals to do anything it asked for the war effort. For the military leaders who wanted to expand Japan's influence, invading China was only the first step.

## Competing Interests in the United States

President Roosevelt, meanwhile, was not receiving much support for his foreign policy goals. During the 1930s, fighting broke out around the world. In Europe, Italy and Germany posed the greatest dangers. Roosevelt saw this, but he also knew that the isolationists at home still wanted to promote peace and avoid tangling the United States in world events, and especially wanted to avoid involvement in another world war.

Even as Japan invaded China and Adolf Hitler invaded Austria and Czechoslovakia, Congress called for nonintervention. Roosevelt was able to win a few concessions from the lawmakers after Germany's surprise invasion of Poland on September 1, 1939. Great Britain and France, allies of the Poles, were soon in the war against Germany, but they could not stop Hitler's progress. By the following summer, the Germans had extended their dominance across most of Western Europe, including France, the Netherlands, and Norway. That summer Italy also joined the war on Hitler's side.

# Good Soldiers, Bad Soldiers

War in China meant jobs for machinists like Kumagaya Tokuichi, who made metal parts used by the Japanese army. Tokuichi, like other Japanese, respected the army and its service for the good of the country:

> They were sacrificing themselves for the country and I felt a sense of gratitude for their hard work. People knew that military duty was as hard as a prison sentence. . . . When I was a boy, all of us in the neighborhood played soldier, using sticks for rifles and swords. Very often, the grown-ups encouraged us to do it. . . . We went to war with light hearts in '37 and '38.

Most Americans, though, saw the Japanese soldiers as cruel, carrying out brutal tactics that went beyond the norms of war. The worst actions came during seven weeks of unrestrained slaughter, a period that has come to be known as the "rape of Nanking." From December 1937 through January 1938, Japanese soldiers in Nanking, then the capital of China, killed 100,000 to 300,000 civilians. The *New York Times* offered a report of the scene:

> *Their [the Japanese] victory was marred, however, by barbaric cruelties, by the wholesale execution of prisoners, the looting of the city, rape, killing of civilians and by general vandalism, which will remain a blot on the reputation of the Japanese Army and the nation. . . . Any person who, through excitement or fear, ran at the approach of the Japanese soldiers was in danger of being shot down.*

Some Japanese officers held beheading competitions with their swords, while soldiers used live prisoners as targets in bayonet drills.

# Ending Neutrality Slowly

On September 3, 1939, President Roosevelt told Americans that the country would remain neutral in the new European war. "But," he added, "I cannot ask that every American remain neutral in thought as well." Fearing that Germany would impose harsh rule across Europe, President Roosevelt wanted to do as much as he could to help the British and French. Noninterventionists, though, spoke out loudly against Roosevelt's efforts to aid the Allies, which were typified by token acts like sending old warships to Great Britain in September 1940. Senator Burton K. Wheeler, a Democrat from Montana, said in December 1940, "I do not believe that the great majority of our people are eager to be embraced by war and I call upon them not to be afraid to say so. I, for one, believe the policy advocated by the interventionists is insane and it will lead to total war, and war is insanity."

In March 1941, despite the feelings of Wheeler and others who opposed intervention, Roosevelt convinced Congress to pass the Lend-Lease Act, which let the British receive supplies without paying for them first. And through 1941, Roosevelt ordered more U.S. Navy ships to patrol the western Atlantic Ocean, where German submarines hunted for British naval and merchant ships. Now convinced of the need to protect the United States from Axis powers bent on world dominance, he told advisers that he wanted war with Germany, but wanted the Nazis to fire the first shot. In August he promised Winston Churchill, prime minister of Great Britain, that he "would wage war, but not declare it, and that he would become more and more provocative." The provocative acts, Roosevelt hoped, would force Germany to attack U.S. forces.

## The Only Way We Can Save Her

In 1939 Casey Orr created this cartoon, which comments that the only way to save Democracy is for the United States to stay out of the European war.

## New Allies, New Challenges

In Japan, military leaders closely watched Hitler's rapid advance in Europe. His gains helped their plans to move southward into British and French colonies and the Dutch East Indies. Some members of the Japanese military began repeating the slogan, "Don't miss the bus!" They meant that the time had come to act, to expand Japanese control in Asia. Great Britain, fighting for its survival, could not focus as closely on defending its colonies. The Netherlands was now under German control and also could barely resist. And with the fall of France, the new pro-German French government allowed Japan to enter Indochina, a region that had been under French control for decades.

Even before Germany's victories in Europe, some Japanese leaders thought they should ally with Adolf Hitler and Italy's Benito Mussolini. The final version of their agreement, the Tripartite Pact, was signed in September 1940. The three nations agreed to help each other "when one of the three contracting powers is attacked by a power at present not involved in the European war or in the Chinese-Japanese conflict." That language targeted the United States, showing how clearly the three Axis nations feared American military potential.

At the time of signing of the Tripartite Pact, Yosuke Matsuoka was Japan's foreign minister. He had studied in the United States and believed he understood how Americans thought. He said the pact would ensure peace. Japan had to "stand firm" so "the American will know he's talking to a man, and you two can then talk man to man." Although most Japanese believed that the United States would not risk a war against their country once it was allied with Germany, certain elements of the military still thought war with America would come.

The increasing Japanese military action was part of its plan to create a "new order" in greater East Asia. The Japanese sought what they called a "co-prosperity sphere" in the region. It was a new name for the old goal of taking the resources it needed from the lands to its south. It also reflected a centuries-old Japanese idea known as *Hakko Ichiu*: "all eight corners of the world under one roof." This was a way of expressing the idea that Japan had a natural right to rule other lands.

After the Tripartite Pact, Roosevelt added more items to an embargo already in place. The embargo prevented the sale of certain U.S. goods, such as scrap metal, that Japan's military could use. Foreign Minister Matsuoka sounded a harsh note in January 1941, saying Japan must "control the western Pacific." The United States should reconsider its efforts to stop that drive, he said, "not only for the sake of Japan, but for the world's sake. And if this request is not heard, there is no hope for Japanese-American relations."

To Japan, seizing oil fields in the Dutch East Indies was the best way to guarantee a steady supply of the precious resource. In July 1941, in preparation for the takeover, the Japanese moved into southern Indochina. U.S. Secretary of State Cordell Hull saw the move as "Japan's last step before jumping off for a full-scale attack in the Southwest Pacific." The Americans responded with a full embargo on oil. Japan had not expected this reaction; rather, it had assumed that the Americans would accept the advance into Indochina.

# Secrets Kept and Revealed

While U.S.–Japanese hostilities were limited to diplomatic moves and countermoves, the United States had a huge advantage. During the 1930s, the Army Signal Intelligence Service (SIS) had broken the code system Japan used to send secret messages to its diplomats overseas. The system was called PURPLE, and the Americans called the decoded messages they received MAGIC. Through 1941 Roosevelt and his top aides knew what Japanese leaders in Tokyo were telling their diplomats in Washington. But the MAGIC messages did not contain actual war plans. Japan's military had ensured that no one outside the highest levels of government would see secret documents discussing contemplated military actions.

Facing the full embargo, Japan's military leaders decided that they would have to go to war to make sure the country had enough fuel. The United States posed the greatest danger for its aggressive plans in Asia.

Roosevelt now insisted that for Japan and the United States to have a normal relationship, Japan had to end its war against China. The Japanese refused. If the Japanese were going to fight, they had to do it soon, before the Americans carried out plans to quickly increase the size of their navy. In Washington, D.C., Japanese diplomats talked of keeping the peace. But the country's military was planning for war.

Despite having broken some Japanese codes, the Americans did not know, in the fall of 1941, that Japan had decided to prepare for war while diplomatic talks went on. If the two countries could not resolve their differences by October 15, the Japanese would attack. But Emperor Hirohito told the military and civilian leaders to try hard to negotiate and prevent war. The leaders agreed, even as some of them personally preferred taking military action. Prime Minister Fumimaro was the main backer of finding a peaceful solution, saying, "We should avoid war against the United States at all costs." But by mid–October, he had lost the support of the army, which favored war. He was replaced by General Hideki Tojo, who was content to allow talks to continue, even as Japan prepared for war.

In his memoirs, written after World War II, Fumimaro reflected the view of many civilian leaders regarding their split with the military—and how that split affected relations with the United States. "In the U.S.–Japanese negotiations," he wrote, "while the government was seriously engaged in the negotiations, the military was furiously making preparations in case of failed negotiations. . . . Naturally, seeing those preparations by our military, the United States did not see any sincerity in our diplomatic efforts."

Even as the military clamored for war, the Japanese government extended the deadline for an American answer to its latest offer until November 25, and then until November 29. Roosevelt and his aides were stalling for time, hoping to build up defenses in the Pacific. From the Japanese perspective, the talks had to reach a positive end soon; otherwise they would need to quickly strike the first blow. Time was not on their side.

Four

# Preparing
# for War

IN THE PERIOD BEFORE the tense negotiations of November 1941, Admiral James O. Richardson commanded the entire U.S. fleet, based in California. In April 1940, he led his ships to Hawaii to conduct sea exercises, expecting to return soon to the shores of the U.S. mainland. But President Roosevelt had other ideas. Through his chief of naval operations (CNO), Admiral Harold R. Stark, he ordered Richardson to keep the entire fleet at Pearl Harbor. The president and his aides believed the presence of the fleet there would deter Japan from carrying out attacks in the Pacific.

Richardson resisted the idea. Keeping his ships and crew supplied would be difficult so far from their California base. Moreover, Hawaii lacked the transportation system and airfields needed to conduct training. Finally, Richardson thought Roosevelt's decision to move the fleet was more about diplomacy than defending the United States. Stark had said as much when he told Richardson that the presence of the fleet in Hawaii might keep the Japanese from attacking the East Indies. To Richardson, the move didn't make military sense. Did the State Department really think, he wondered, that the fleet "could embark on a campaign

A Japanese photographer took this photo minutes before the attack on Pearl Harbor. It clearly shows American ships clustered together in the harbor.

directly from Hawaii or safely conduct necessary training . . . at Lahaina [in Hawaii] which is 2,000 miles nearer enemy submarine bases than our normal Pacific Coast bases?"

In the months that followed, Richardson argued his case for moving the fleet back to California. But Stark, the CNO, and the civilian leaders would not budge. Richardson also disagreed with Stark on the appropriate way to defend the fleet while at Pearl Harbor. For example, Richardson didn't see the need to place torpedo nets in the harbor, since this measure was designed to stop enemy torpedoes from reaching the ships and he didn't think Japan would attack the fleet by dropping torpedoes from aircraft. Nets were later used, however, to keep enemy subs out of the harbor.

As a result of his arguments with his superiors, Richardson was replaced on February 1, 1941. Thereafter, Admiral Husband E. Kimmel would help shape defenses at Pearl Harbor as his government and the Japanese continued their diplomacy. But even while talks went on, some Japanese leaders deepened their preparations for war.

## Choosing Pearl Harbor

At almost the same time Kimmel took command of the U.S. fleet in Hawaii, Admiral Isoroku Yamamoto was readying a war plan he had first devised months before. Yamamoto was Japan's best naval officer and commanded the country's entire fleet. In both Japan and the United States, he was considered one of the greatest naval minds of his generation. He was known both for his intelligence and for his willingness to gamble—and he knew that an attack on Pearl Harbor would be a huge gamble. Yamamoto had spent time in the United States as a student at Harvard University in Cambridge, Massachusetts, and as a naval attaché in Washington, D.C. He knew the country's industrial strength. In the months before the attack, he often feared that war with the United States would crush Japan. But he was given the task of planning for war, and he came up with the surprise attack on Pearl Harbor.

Admiral Isoroku Yamamoto was the mastermind behind the Japanese attack on Pearl Harbor.

Earlier Japanese naval commanders had assumed that if war came with the United States, the two navies would fight at sea. Yamamoto believed that Japan had to strike at the U.S. fleet before it reached open waters. He wrote, "We should do our best to decide the fate of the war on the very first day." A massive first strike, catching the U.S. forces off guard, would stun the Americans. Yamamoto hoped that the shock and the loss of most of its Pacific fleet would weaken the will of the United States to wage and win a war. The admiral had reservations, however. In January 1941, he wrote that taking Pearl Harbor, or even San Francisco, would not be enough to ensure a Japanese victory. "To make victory certain, we would have to march into Washington and dictate the terms of peace in the White House." In fact, Yamamoto went further. Many Americans today are surprised to learn of the admiral's doubts that his country's leaders had the will to make the sacrifices such an effort would take.

A model of Pearl Harbor was constructed in Japan and used by Japanese pilots during their preparation and training for the attack.

# The January Rumor

Joseph Grew became the U.S. ambassador to Japan in 1932. His wife was the granddaughter of Matthew Perry, the American naval commander who had opened Japan to the West. When President Roosevelt first took office, Grew described Japan's growing military might. He looked for ways to improve U.S.– Japanese relations, but by January 1941 he saw a growing threat. "Japan, not we, is on the warpath." Just a few weeks later, he reported a rumor he had heard from another diplomat, warning of a possible attack on Pearl Harbor. The source did not believe the rumor, Grew wrote to Washington. Still, "the fact that he had heard it from many sources prompted him to pass on the information." U.S. Naval Intelligence ignored the report, saying that based on its knowledge of Japan's military preparations, "no move against Pearl Harbor appears imminent or planned for the foreseeable future."

Yamamoto assembled the pieces for his Pearl Harbor attack while U.S. and Japanese diplomats tried to heal the growing split between their countries. Other admirals offered their ideas, building on Yamamoto's basic concept. The attack should target U.S. aircraft carriers and planes on the ground, not just battleships. Japan should send the largest force possible of its own carriers to stage the attack, using every bombing method available: dive-bombing, launching torpedo bombs, and high-altitude bombing. It was essential to have plenty of fighter planes to defend the bombers and, since the Japanese were not skilled in nighttime bombing, a daylight attack was necessary, as well. Perhaps most important of all, the plan would have to be developed and initiated in complete secrecy.

Not all Japanese naval commanders supported Yamamoto's plan, which came to be called Operation Z. These commanders thought the naval resources being directed toward the Pearl Harbor attack were weakening Japan's military efforts in East Asia. And what if the Japanese fleet reached its target and no American ships were there? Despite his grave doubts about the wisdom of starting a war with the United States, however, Yamamoto did not doubt the workability of his plan, should he be ordered to carry out a first strike. In the face of the criticism, he was prepared to give up his command if Tokyo halted Operation Z.

## Pearl Harbor Prepares

Meanwhile, halfway around the world in Washington, U.S. military leaders considered the future. They couldn't predict exactly what Japan might do if war came, so they had to prepare for a variety of situations. Upon taking command of the fleet at Pearl Harbor, Admiral Kimmel found a dangerous situation. He thought a surprise attack of some kind was a possibility. U.S. war games a few years before had indicated that an enemy with sufficient carrier-based aircraft could heavily damage the big military installation.

One possible defense was to send more warplanes to Oahu, and in April 1941 military planners in Washington called for this to be done. At almost the same time, Roosevelt cut the size of the fleet at Pearl Harbor, sending ships to the Atlantic to face the threat from German submarines, or U-boats. Kimmel felt that his loss of ships made Japan even more likely to go to war, since he would have less firepower at sea to deter or stop any attack. The president, meanwhile, was focused more intently than ever on the war against Germany.

Kimmel was not the only commander at Pearl Harbor concerned about a surprise attack. Lieutenant General Walter C. Short was in charge of defending the island and the various military bases there. In August 1941, after barely seven months on the job, he had concluded that an attack by air was "not impossible and in certain situations it might not be improbable."

For Short, the major task was protecting the fleet. The ships were especially vulnerable, for to reach the open sea in the event of an attack, they would have to pass one by one through a narrow channel. To accomplish this quickly, under emergency conditions, would be very challenging. Yet Short saw the fleet as the major block to an attack by Japan. As he said afterward, "I would have been much more worried if there had been no fleet in Hawaiian waters." To Short, the presence of the fleet meant that even if he could not rule out an attack, Japan would be less likely to strike with all those ships in place. Yet others saw this as flawed thinking, since the ships were the only targets at Oahu truly worth hitting.

During the fall of 1941, both Kimmel and Short had their men preparing for war, sometimes training together. Planes also carried out reconnaissance, looking for signs of the Japanese, though Kimmel and Short lacked the aircraft they needed to search far in every direction. Short also later complained that his men didn't have enough artillery to fully protect the island. Still, as late as October 20, Short believed the assurance he had received from Washington: "they did not expect any abrupt change in the relations between the United States and Japan."

## The Crisis Deepens

But in the month that followed, the diplomatic efforts to prevent war began to crumble. Through November, Secretary of State Hull met with Japanese diplomat Kichisaburo Nomura, who made offers that called for the Americans to end the embargo on oil sales and for talks to end the war between China and Japan. Roosevelt rejected these proposals, but he was encouraged that Japan was trying to seek a peaceful solution. He and Hull began writing their own proposals for peace. Through MAGIC, however, Roosevelt knew time was running out. Japan would strike if the two countries did not reach an agreement by November 29.

Roosevelt told aides that it was important to make Japan fire the first shot "without allowing too much danger to ourselves." Roosevelt knew he would win overwhelming support from Congress only if Japan struck U.S. targets, as opposed to British or Dutch possessions. Neither the

Americans nor the British knew exactly where Japan would strike. The Philippines, the Dutch East Indies, and British colonies in Asia were all possible targets. So was Pearl Harbor, though its distance from Japan seemed to make it a less likely choice. In the end, Japan made daring attacks on all these targets, nearly simultaneously.

On November 26, 1941, Roosevelt, through Secretary Hull, gave Japan his own proposal for continuing talks. It called for Japan to remove all its troops from China and Indochina and pull out of the Tripartite Pact. No deadline was given for compliance, and there was no threat of U.S. action if Japan rejected the offer. But Nomura considered the proposal an insulting demand for major concessions from his country.

Other Japanese leaders felt the same way and considered the talks over. Some saw the U.S. proposal as an ultimatum—if Japan rejected the "Hull Note," the Americans might strike first. The emperor and his advisers did not know of Roosevelt's determination not to fire the first shot. To some Japanese military officers, the note demanding that Japan cease its aggression in Asia as the price of good relations with the United States was the last straw. A diplomatic message from Tokyo to its embassy in Berlin said, "It is clear that the United States . . . has decided to regard Japan, along with Germany and Italy, as an enemy." Japan would go to war—and the officers welcomed it. But the Tojo government told Nomura to act as if peace could still be preserved. Once again, MAGIC told Roosevelt what Japan really intended. He knew Japan would strike, but he still did not know where or when.

# A Fleet at Sea

Also on November 26 (November 25 in Japan: the dates
are different because Japan and the United States are on
opposite sides of the International Date Line, the imaginary
line that runs north to south on the planet and is the basis
for the world's twenty-four time zones), a Japanese fleet
sailed from the Kurile Islands, north of the main Japanese
islands. Its commander, Chuichi Nagumo, was prepared to
follow Yamamoto's plan for attacking Pearl Harbor. Four
days later, Roosevelt learned that a Japanese fleet was sailing south from China. But Nagumo's ships had not been
detected at the early stages of their long voyage to Hawaii.
Japanese subs, which had sailed even earlier in the month,
were also making their way eastward across the Pacific. Yet
to the Americans and their allies, British or Dutch territory
still seemed the most likely Japanese target.

Before sailing, Nagumo and other Japanese naval commanders had received "Top Secret Operation Order No. 1."
In it, Yamamoto outlined the strategy for war, if it came. He
also wrote, "When Britain and America have been driven from
the Netherland Indies and the Philippines, an independent,
self-supporting economic entity will be firmly established.
The vast and far-reaching fundamental principle, the goal of
our nation—*Hakko Ichiu*—will be demonstrated to the world."

On November 29, the last Japanese deadline passed.
Given the failure of the talks, Tojo soon said, Japan had no
choice but to "begin war . . . in order to resolve the present
crisis and assure survival." To the Japanese leaders, British
and American policies threatened to weaken, if not destroy,
Japan. War was the only honorable answer. But even as they
began war, some of Japan's leaders feared how it would end.

# The Decision for War

The final Japanese decision to go to war came on December 2, 1941. Military and civilian leaders met with Emperor Hirohito to explain the situation. Here are some of the views Hirohito heard:

Foreign Minister Shigenori Togo: "I believe that America's policy toward Japan has consistently been to thwart the establishment of a New Order in East Asia, which is our immutable [unchangeable] policy . . . if we were to accept their present proposal . . . our very survival would inevitably be threatened."

Prime Minister for Home Affairs Hideki Tojo: "The people in general are aware that our nation, in view of the present world situation, stands at a crossroads, one road leading to glory and the other to decline . . . they are truly determined to undergo all manner of hardships, and to overcome adversity by united action."

President of the Privy Council, Yoshimichi Hara: "The United States is being utterly conceited, obstinate, and disrespectful. . . . We simply cannot tolerate such an attitude."

The person taking notes at the meeting observed that the emperor "nodded in agreement with the statements being made, and displayed no signs of uneasiness."

# Five

# Caught
# Off Guard

NOVEMBER 1941 saw concerns increase in both Hawaii and Washington, D.C. But Admiral Kimmel and General Short didn't know the full extent of the trouble brewing. They took actions based on the messages they received from Washington. Kimmel relied on Admiral Stark, while Short reported to Stark's counterpart, General George C. Marshall, the army chief of staff. Neither Washington official gave Kimmel and Short full details of the MAGIC messages. The two commanders in Hawaii didn't know that Japanese leaders seemed to be ready to fight once the November 29 deadline passed.

On November 24, Admiral Kimmel and other Pacific commanders received a clear message from Washington: that a surprise attack was possible from any direction. The message specifically mentioned the Philippines and Guam as possible targets—but not Pearl Harbor.

More ominous messages from Washington came on November 27. Both Kimmel and Short were told that talks with Japan had failed and a "hostile action" or "aggressive move" could come at any moment. Once again, though, Pearl Harbor was not mentioned as a specific target. Short's message instructed him to begin reconnaissance and prepare his defenses, but not to take any actions that would alarm civilians at Oahu or signal preparations for war. Kimmel's message was called a "war warning." His intelligence officer, Lieutenant Commander Edwin Layton, said reading the message "gave me a jolt." But he didn't think Hawaii was at risk.

Kimmel and Short exchanged the messages they received. Short told his men to prepare for sabotage, which had been one of his major worries. He assumed that some Japanese Americans on the island would support Japan and would try to damage U.S. weapons and military supplies. When not flying, planes were grouped close together on the ground so they could be easily defended. Ammunition was locked away to prevent theft. Defending against sabotage was the lowest level of readiness for war on a three-part scale Short had devised.

The general soon told Washington the steps he had taken. But he had not begun reconnaissance, thinking Kimmel would take care of it. Kimmel, for his part, thought Short was preparing for an all-out attack, not merely for sabotage. Although both assumptions were wrong, the two commanders did agree that Hawaii wasn't the likely target and that sabotage was the most pressing danger.

In the days that followed, Kimmel learned that Naval Intelligence could no longer locate the Japanese carriers the agency had been tracking at sea; Layton told him the ships were probably still close to their bases in Japan. Kimmel grew upset as he realized the ships could be almost anywhere in the Pacific, and no Americans knew where. Within a few days, Layton suggested that the "missing" ships were probably on their way to Thailand and other destinations in Asia.

# The Fleet Approaches

At sea, Admiral Nagumo's ships continued to steam toward Hawaii, now under radio silence, which the admiral maintained by using signal flags and lights to communicate with his ships. The sailors didn't even throw their garbage overboard, as they usually did, so there would be no trail in the water for other ships to see. Secrecy and surprise were the keys to Operation Z, and the order for radio silence explains why U.S. intelligence had lost track of the attacking fleet. The ships, though, could still receive messages from Tokyo, and on December 2, Admiral Yamamoto sent this signal: *"Niita-kayama nobore"* ["Climb Mount Niitaka"]. The coded message meant that the attack was on for December 8, which would be December 7 in the United States because, again, of the International Date Line.

The major part of Japan's Pearl Harbor Strike Force consisted of six aircraft carriers and their hundreds of planes. Beside them were twenty more ships, including battleships and heavy cruisers. The vessels had first sailed eastward far to the north of Hawaii. Then, on December 6, they turned southward, increasing their speed. They took dead aim at Oahu, though they would stay about 200 miles away from the target, to allow the carriers to launch their planes.

Also at sea, separate from the Pearl Harbor Strike Task Force, was a fleet of Japanese submarines. They approached Oahu from different directions, and by December 6 some were only 8 miles from Pearl Harbor. Several carried mini-subs that would sneak into the harbor, wait for the aerial assault, and then launch their torpedoes. The sailors on the minisubs knew they faced great danger. If they were discovered by U.S. forces, they would have no way of defending

The strike on Pearl Harbor was supported by six Japanese aircraft carriers, plus battleships, cruisers, and hundreds of planes.

themselves. The sailors actually took pride in their willingness to die, as Admiral Matome Ugaki noted. "How much damage they will be able to inflict is not the point. The firm determination not to return alive on the part of those . . . who smilingly embarked on their ships cannot be praised too much. The spirit of *kesshitai* [self-sacrifice] has not changed at all." (The Japanese culture valued willingness to sacrifice oneself for the good of the nation.)

The Americans had planned a defense against enemy subs — nets strung underwater across the harbor. The mini-subs, in turn, were equipped with special cutters on their bows to slice through the nets the Japanese expected to find.

# Advanced Technology

U.S. Ambassador Joseph Grew and others had written about the strength of the Japanese military. But some U.S. officials underestimated their technological skills. They didn't know about the new tools the Japanese had developed to wage war. The minisubs used at Pearl Harbor were just one example. Powered by diesel electricity, they were twice as fast as any U.S. sub of the day. One later Japanese sub, built during the war, was large enough to carry two bomber planes that could be launched when the vessel had surfaced.

The British had done something similar the year before, for a devastating attack on Italian ships docked at Taranto, Italy. The water at Pearl Harbor was too shallow for normal torpedoes. The Japanese added small wooden fins to theirs, which helped them stay close to the surface. Before December 7, however, U.S. military officials had shared the thinking of Pearl Harbor survivor Leon Kolb, who later said, "I never dreamed that torpedo planes could attack the harbor."

Japanese pilots receive instructions aboard an aircraft carrier before their attack on Pearl Harbor.

But the cutters proved to be unnecessary at Pearl Harbor. Two of the five subs reached the harbor and found the nets open: no one had closed them after a recent passage by a U.S. ship.

A few hours after midnight, farther out at sea, the pilots on the Japanese aircraft carriers prepared for battle. They wore hand-sewn belts that served as good-luck charms, and they ate a special meal of rice and fish. The seas were rough that day, and normally the planes would not have launched under those conditions. But now nothing was going to stop Operation Z.

## Messages Sent and Missed

In the days before December 7, messages the Americans decoded seemed to indicate that something was about to happen in the Pacific. Japanese diplomats at different international posts, including Hawaii, received instructions to destroy important papers. This action is common when war breaks out, to prevent the enemy from seizing documents containing crucial information. In Hawaii, U.S. intelligence officials were listening in on phone lines at Japan's diplomatic offices in Honolulu. They knew when the order to destroy papers arrived, but Admiral Kimmel didn't hear about it until December 6. He had received similar reports before, so he didn't interpret the news to mean that Pearl Harbor faced immediate danger.

Unfortunately for the United States, Kimmel also had not heard of earlier MAGIC reports suggesting that Japan was carefully watching the movement of his ships. Spies on the island, however, had been reporting which of the U.S. ships were at sea. If Kimmel had known this, and had been told earlier that Japanese diplomats were destroying important papers, he might have taken more forceful action, such as sending his remaining ships to sea, or discussing stronger defensive actions with General Short. But from what both commanders knew, the real threat of war was thousands of miles away, in the Philippines or in the British and Dutch colonies.

## Messages in Washington

On December 6 and 7, various messages came in and went out of U.S. government offices. President Roosevelt still hoped to avoid war. He was still waiting for the official Japanese response to the Hull Note of November 26. The president sent a personal message to Emperor Hirohito. He called the buildup of Japanese forces in Indochina and the threat they posed a "keg of dynamite." He asked Hirohito to remove the troops, which would result in an "assurance of peace throughout the whole of the South Pacific area."

Starting that evening, Roosevelt received new MAGIC messages with instructions from Japan to its diplomats in the United States. When the last part arrived on the morning of December 7, the message stated what most U.S. leaders had already guessed: Japan would no longer negotiate. As everything had been indicating for some time, Japan was now likely to make its military move. The Americans, however, still didn't know exactly when and where. Pearl Harbor still didn't seem like a likely target, and if it were, it wouldn't matter—or so the military commanders in Washington thought. They assumed that Kimmel had sent his ships out to sea after the earlier war warning. The carriers based there had already departed on a mission to bring planes to Wake Island and Midway, U.S. possessions farther out in the Pacific. A third was on its way to Pearl Harbor but was slowed by bad weather. So of the country's major warships, only the battleships sat at their docks.

General George C. Marshall finally decided to send another warning message to army commanders stationed in the Pacific, including General Short on Oahu. Marshall could have called on a special high-security phone, but he decided not to risk using it in case the Japanese had some way of listening. The message went out over a slower form of radio communication. By the time General Short received the new warning, later in the afternoon, Hawaii time, it was too late.

## TORA, TORA, TORA

War was in the air in Washington and Tokyo, but Pearl Harbor was a fairly peaceful spot in the days before December 7. Even when a new report reached Layton on December 6 about Japanese activity in the Pacific, some U.S. officers weren't worried. Vice Admiral William Pye said, "The Japanese will not go to war with the United States. We are too big, too powerful, and too strong."

December 6 was a fairly normal Saturday for the people of Pearl Harbor. Ruth Erickson, a navy nurse, worked a regular shift and looked forward to the next day off. On that Sunday morning, enjoying a cup of coffee, she and some other nurses heard planes buzzing over a small island in the harbor. Then, noises they didn't recognize made them jump from their chairs and head to the windows. Erikson later said, "There was a plane flying directly over the top of our quarters, a one-story structure. The rising sun under the wing of the plane denoted the enemy. . . . My heart was racing, the telephone was ringing, the chief nurse, Gertrude Arnest, was saying, 'Girls, get into your uniforms at once. This is the real thing!'"

Future U.S. senator Daniel Inouye was a high schooler on Oahu on that Sunday morning. He woke to see that the sun had already burned off the morning haze, forecasting a beautiful day. But then he heard the radio bulletin announcing an enemy attack, and he went outside to see the advancing Japanese planes. He later wrote, "They came zooming out of that sea of gray smoke, flying north toward where we stood and climbing into the bluest part of the sky."

# First Reports

In an age before television and computers, radio broadcasts gave millions of Americans their first news of the Pearl Harbor attack. Then newspapers quickly put out special editions, offering more details.

Here is an excerpt from an early U.S. news report on the attack, from the *Providence* [Rhode Island] *Journal*:

> At least two Japanese bombers . . . appeared over Honolulu at about 7:35 AM (Honolulu time) today and dropped bombs. . . . The sound of cannon firing comes to me here in Honolulu, as I telephone this story to the San Francisco Associated Press office. Reports say that the Japanese bombers scored two hits, one at Hickam Field, Air Corps Post on Oahu Island, and another at Pearl Harbor, setting an oil tank afire.

In Japan, meanwhile, Prime Minister Hideki Tojo made the announcement on radio that Japan had declared war on the United States and Great Britain. A *New York Times* article offered highlights of Tojo's radio address to his people: "Japan has done her utmost to prevent this war, but in self-protection and for self-existence we could not help declaring war— considering the past attitude and acts of the United States. . . . I hereby promise you that the final victory will be that of Japan . . . there is nothing [for Japanese civilians] to fear in this war."

A view of Pearl Harbor from the hills above captures antiaircraft shells bursting overhead and the destruction of the USS *Arizona* (large column of smoke in the center).

The two waves of Japanese attacks threw all of Oahu into a frenzy. In the harbor, some sailors manned guns, aiming at the Japanese aircraft swooping overhead. Others prepared their ships to sail, the commanders hoping to leave port and avoid destruction. Several destroyers did manage to escape. Fred Lowrey, a resident of Oahu, watched the action unfold through a telescope. "I saw ships trying to get out [to sea] . . . I saw planes above. I saw plumes of water jump in the air where bombs had hit alongside of the ships, [spouting] fifty to a hundred feet in the air. And then as I turned the telescope further mauka [inland], I could see the fires at [Hickam and] Pearl Harbor."

At the airfields, firefighters tried to douse the flames of U.S. planes burning in their hangars. Japanese Zeros, flying low and firing their machine guns, made the job almost impossible. Some sailors grabbed rifles and fired at the incoming fighters, ignoring how overmatched they were. The spreading fires and blasts from bombs sent thick smoke billowing over the harbor.

Even with the smoke, the Japanese pilots knew they had done their job well. After the attack, Commander Sadamu Sanagi wrote in his diary, praising the entire Japanese Navy: "This success is owing to the Imperial Navy's hard training for more than twenty years. . . . Nothing could hold back our Imperial Navy . . . it never hesitated to dare to do the most difficult thing on this Earth. Oh, how powerful is the Imperial Navy!" But to Edwin Layton, the fires and destruction and death were like "a bad dream that could not be true."

Secretary of State Hull learned of the attack just after 2 p.m. He was preparing to meet the Japanese diplomats, who were late for their meeting to deliver Japan's last diplomatic message. They had no idea that Hull already knew the contents of the message—and that their country had just attacked the United States. Hull didn't share the explosive information, however, and the Japanese diplomats seemed puzzled by his angry attitude. They soon learned why Hull was so upset, as they found out for the first time about the successful surprise attack on Pearl Harbor.

# Six

# Anger and Pride, Fear and Accusations

PEARL HARBOR WAS NOT THE ONLY Japanese target on December 7. Soon after the Hawaii raid, the Japanese attacked the Malay Peninsula and Hong Kong, which were under British control. Then, after the first bombs fell on Hawaii, Japanese planes struck U.S. bases at the Philippines, and later they attacked the Pacific islands of Wake and Guam. Word then went out to U.S. Navy commanders across the Pacific: "Execute unrestricted air and submarine warfare against Japan."

## Americans React

With each side officially declaring war on the other, and Germany and Italy soon entering on Japan's side, average citizens on both sides of the Pacific reacted to what was now truly a second world war.

The news of Pearl Harbor had stunned Edward Osberg, a resident of the Midwest. He was eating Sunday dinner with his family on December 7 when he heard the report: "I was an avid reader of the newspapers and had seen the portents [signs] that something was going to explode somewhere, but I didn't know how or when, and, of course, I didn't

William Green, president of the American Federation of Labor, puts up signs on December 9, 1941, urging labor workers to cooperate in the defense program.

expect Pearl Harbor. When it came, it was a tremendous shock."

Dellie Hahne was a college student in California when she heard about the attack on Pearl Harbor. She felt a "hideous fear that the bombers would come and we'd all be killed. It was a horrible moment." But she also saw other college students realize the importance of the event. "'The Star-Spangled Banner' was played, and everyone in the room automatically rose. . . . The outward show of patriotism was something that I had always sneered at, but we all stood and we all tingled. So the fervor started right off the bat. It was like a disease, and we all caught it." Patriotism seemed to overwhelm most American isolationists, too. The America First Committee, one of the largest nonintervention groups, quickly shut down.

A few days after December 7, the *New York Times* captured the mood in the country's largest city, a mood shared across the United States: "The people . . . received the news that we are at war . . . with profound calm and a quiet, stern determination to see it through, no matter how long it takes." Many Americans could think only of revenge. But Carroll Alcott, a journalist who had worked in Japan, said the war should not be about revenge. To him, war with Japan had been inevitable—the same thing some Japanese military planners had said for years. Japan had "the desire, possibly the necessity . . . to expand its domain at the expense of others." The United States faced its own necessity—preventing Japan from achieving that goal. Americans, Alcott asserted, "are facing the most ruthless and determined foe they have encountered in all their history."

## Reaction in Japan

In Japan, war had been a way of life since 1937. Taking on new military actions against the United States, and Britain as well, would present enormous challenges. But many Japanese had faith in their military, and in their country's destiny. They accepted the principle of *Hakko Ichiu* and believed Japan was a special nation, with a special and dominant role to play in Asia. Fighting the Americans and British was part of that role.

Nogi Harumichi was a college student with strong nationalist beliefs. He supported Japan's efforts to build the Co-Prosperity Sphere in East Asia. When he heard about Pearl Harbor, he thought, "What was supposed to happen had finally taken place. I felt a sense of relief at that moment more than anything else. . . . Suddenly the constraints of deadlock were broken and the way before Japan was cleared."

A few years younger than Harumichi, Itabashi Kōshū heard the news of the war on the radio. "I felt as if my blood boiled and my flesh quivered. The whole nation bubbled over, excited and inspired. 'We really did it! Incredible! Wonderful!' That's the way it felt then . . . the whole nation was at war, everyone was for the war."

Actually, not everyone was for the war. Some Japanese military officers and political leaders knew America's industrial strength. People who had struggled to prevent the war, such as Konoe Fumimaro, now worried for the future of Japan. On New Year's Day, just weeks after the attack on Pearl Harbor, he attended a party at the Imperial Palace. Members of the government bubbled with joy. Fumimaro told a friend, "It is almost unbelievable that these old folks

# A Teacher's View

Ienaga Saburō was a teacher in Niigata, Japan, when Pearl Harbor was attacked. He later became one of his country's greatest historians. Here he reflects on his feelings when the war began:

> I knew, in general terms, how great the national strength of Britain and the United States really was. I knew instinctively that to fight America and England simultaneously made no sense. . . . When I heard the news of the opening of the war on December 8, I experienced a sense of desperation. From that time on, I simply wished that the war would end, even one day early, but I couldn't do anything to help bring that about. . . . I must take that responsibility for simply standing by and watching the war go on.

are truly convinced that Japan will keep on winning and actually be victorious in this war."

## Opposing the War

In both the United States and Japan, most people rallied around their government and the military after Pearl Harbor. But in each country, some people actively opposed the war, for various reasons.

In the United States, pacifists, who opposed all wars, spoke out against the idea of Americans' fighting in World War II, even after Pearl Harbor. One pacifist was Jeannette Rankin, a member of the U.S. House of Representatives. She cast the only vote opposing Roosevelt's call for Congress to declare war against Japan.

Many pacifists' views were shaped by their religious beliefs. Dorothy Day helped publish a newspaper called the *Catholic Worker*. Her faith led her to oppose all wars. Catholic teachings supported the idea of "just wars," which included a country defending itself when it was attacked. But Day, noting that modern technology had created weapons that made it too hard to prevent massive civilian deaths, believed that the just-war concept should be forgotten. In January 1942, an editorial in the *Catholic Worker* said, "We are still pacifists . . . which means we will try to be peacemakers."

In Japan, an outlawed political party was the only group to actively protest the war. Japan's leaders opposed the Communist Party, which called for government ownership of most private property and the end of militarism. One woman, a teacher named Hasegawa Teru, who was living in China, spoke out against all of Japan's wars of aggression. But in general, few Japanese publicly objected to the war

Interned Japanese wait in front of the camp office after arriving at Manzanar.

against the Allied powers, knowing they would face arrest —
or worse — if they did.

## An American Threat?

In the weeks after Pearl Harbor, rumors spread about more
Japanese attacks on the United States, and some Americans
questioned the loyalty of Japanese Americans, especially
those on the West Coast. Despite having received a report
that few Japanese Americans posed any danger, President
Roosevelt approved a plan to send Japanese Americans living
on the mainland to special restricted areas called relocation
centers. They came to be known as internment camps. Even
U.S. citizens of Japanese origin were forced to leave their
homes, sell most of their belongings, and head to the camps.
The government of Canada did the same thing to Japanese

Canadians, as fear of Japan gripped all of western North America.

War with Japan stirred some real fears of sabotage or spying by Japanese agents already in the country. But Roosevelt's sending more than 110,000 Japanese Americans to the camps was largely fueled by fear of the unknown and of Japanese military power, as well as by racism, which Japanese Americans had felt before.

That racism had first led many Americans to believe that Japan could not carry out as sophisticated an attack as the one on Pearl Harbor. John Grove, a Californian, summed up the view at the time: "Because most prewar Japanese exports of manufactured goods to this country were shoddy imitations of quality U.S. or European articles, it was not surprising that Americans felt that 'Jap' ships, planes, tanks and guns were of poor quality . . . another example [of racism] was an article in a respected U.S. aviation magazine in the summer of 1941 which declared that Japanese military pilots would have no chance against our pilots because all Japanese had poor eyesight."

But if the Americans had once dismissed Japan's fighting ability, after Pearl Harbor they stressed the supposedly "sneaky" nature of the Japanese and feared that Japanese Americans would be disloyal. California lawmaker Leland Ford wrote a letter to the federal government calling for a close watch over Japanese Americans. "I do not believe we could be any too strict in our consideration of the Japanese in the face of the treacherous way in which they do things."

While Ford was concerned with Japanese Americans on the mainland, some military officials worried about the Japanese in Hawaii, where they made up about one-third of

# Camp Life

Jeanne Wakatsuki and her family were sent to an internment camp in Manzanar, California, an isolated spot near the Sierra Nevada range. Years later, the woman wrote about her experiences in the camp. Here is part of her autobiography:

*I don't remember what we ate that first morning. I know we stood for half an hour in cutting wind waiting to get our food. Then we took it back to the cubicle and ate huddled around the stove. . . . I was sick continually, with stomach cramps and diarrhea. At first it was from the shots they gave us for typhoid . . . that knocked all of us younger kids down at once, with fevers and vomiting. Later, it was the food that made us sick, young and old alike. . . . Food would spoil from being left out too long. That summer, when the heat got fierce, it would spoil faster. . . . The Manzanar runs became a condition of life, and you only hoped that when you rushed to the latrine [toilet], one would be in working order.*

the population. An early plan to intern them was scrapped. They were needed to help rebuild Pearl Harbor and keep Hawaii's economy running. Only about a thousand Japanese Americans, most considered possible troublemakers, were taken off the islands. But on the West Coast, Japanese Americans were not as essential to the war effort. Sending them away would not affect the economy. Indeed, some American farmers hoped to take over land their Japanese American neighbors were forced to abandon.

At the internment camps, some Japanese Americans lived behind barbed wire for several years. Before reaching their final assigned spot, some of the internees were forced to stay at temporary camps set up at racetracks. They slept in smelly stalls that once housed horses. At the internment camps, some Japanese Americans got sick from eating spoiled food and endured extremes of cold and heat. They lost their privacy, their legal rights, and their freedom.

## Questioning the Camps

Japan's leaders immediately denounced the relocation of Japanese Americans, especially those who were U.S. citizens. Speaking for the government, Radio Tokyo called the relocation "diabolic savagery" and said, "The viciousness of the American Government in persecuting a helpless, strictly civilian and manifestly innocent minority will remain in history as one of the blackest crimes ever committed by the so-called great powers." History records, however, that as the Japanese made these charges, they were keeping Allied prisoners of war in much worse prison camps, killing and maiming some of them. And the brutal treatment of civilians, begun in China, continued as Japan advanced through

Southeast Asia. The internees in the U.S. camps did not face punitive actions as harsh as those routinely used in Asia.

Still, some of Roosevelt's aides also opposed the internment program even as many politicians from western states and some military officers supported it. Over time, though, the military saw the value of having some soldiers who could speak Japanese working in noncombat positions. And Roosevelt saw the value of challenging the notion, spread by Japan, that all Americans were racists. He decided that U.S. citizens of Japanese descent could volunteer for the military if they passed a special loyalty test. They were not, however, allowed to fight in Asia. About a thousand young Japanese American men left the camps to fight in Europe. They were joined by Japanese American volunteers from Hawaii. Their units won praise for their bravery and helped prove the loyalty of Japanese Americans.

A small number of Americans opposed the camps on legal grounds, especially when the internees were U.S. citizens. The American Civil Liberties Union helped a few Japanese Americans challenge the camps in court. The internees lost several cases decided by the U.S. Supreme Court, but finally won a favorable decision in 1944. In *Ex Parte Mitsuye Endo*, the Court ruled that the government did not have the right to detain U.S. citizens who were not threats to the country's security. Justice William O. Douglas wrote, "A citizen who is concededly loyal presents no problem of espionage or sabotage. Loyalty is a matter of the heart and mind not of race, creed, or color. He who is loyal is by definition not a spy or a saboteur."

## Placing Blame

Along with fear and hatred of the Japanese, the Pearl Harbor attack stirred a desire by some Americans to learn what had gone wrong. How had the military been so unprepared for assault? Some lawmakers wanted to know who, if anyone, was to blame for being caught off guard at Pearl Harbor.

On December 11, Republican senator Charles Tobey of New Hampshire called for an investigation of what happened in Hawaii in the days leading up to the attack. Senator David Walsh of Massachusetts, a Democrat, challenged Tobey. Walsh said the country had to trust Roosevelt, who was now a "war president." Walsh believed that "[I]f there was carelessness . . . if there was failure to prepare for what took place on that fateful Sunday morning, the Commander in Chief must, and I believe he will, put his hands upon it and act in such a manner that he will receive the confidence of the American people."

Roosevelt wanted full support from Congress and the American people as he tried to lead the country through a war being fought on two fronts, Europe and Asia. He knew the difficulties ahead, and he knew some sort of investigation was needed. The president immediately sent Secretary of the Navy Frank Knox to Hawaii to speak to Admiral Kimmel and General Short. In a private report, Knox wrote that on the basis of information received, the two commanders hadn't believed they would be attacked.

Still facing criticism from Republicans, Roosevelt ordered a second investigation. He chose Owen J. Roberts, an associate justice of the U.S. Supreme Court, to lead a commission, which included four military officers. After about one month of investigations, the Roberts Commission said that none of Roosevelt's top advisers in Washington were to blame for the attack. Quite unfairly, the report laid blame on the local commanders. It said that Kimmel and Short "failed properly to evaluate the seriousness of the situation. These errors of judgment were the effective causes for the success of the attack."

Although Kimmel and Short took most of the blame and were removed from their posts, some Americans thought the real blame lay in Washington—perhaps in the White House itself. Calls to discover the truth behind Pearl Harbor increased, even as the fighting went on.

# Seven
# Struggle for Victory — and Truth

THE YEARS AFTER PEARL HARBOR were difficult for Americans, both at home and overseas. Civilians were forced to cut back on their use of fuel, as well as some foods, such as meat, so these valuable commodities could be used for the war effort. The troops on the front lines faced harsh living conditions and the constant danger of injury or death. Americans captured by Japanese troops were often tortured or killed. But as Roosevelt hoped, the country had united in the effort to fight militaristic nations. In 1944 he praised Americans for meeting "the demands of this war with magnificent courage and understanding." Yet the president knew that some Americans still opposed his policies. And some still wondered what had happened before Pearl Harbor. They were not satisfied that Kimmel and Short were the only ones to blame.

One of those who were reluctant to place the entire blame on Kimmel and Short was Laurence Safford, a captain in Naval Intelligence. Safford had remembered seeing a message on December 4, 1941, that contained a secret Japanese code for carrying out a surprise attack. The Americans already knew the Japanese would use a code describing the direction of the wind to signal if Japan were going to war. The December 4 "winds execute" message indicated that Great Britain and the United States would be the target. Safford believed many other officers had also seen the message.

In 1944 Safford told Kimmel his thoughts. The admiral went to several members of Congress who thought the truth about the surprise attack was still unknown. Soon the lawmakers required the army and the navy to begin new hearings on the events leading up to Pearl Harbor.

The hearings began in July 1944 and ran through October. Altogether, the Navy Court of Inquiry and the Army Pearl Harbor Board heard from several hundred witnesses. The naval court found that based on what he knew, Kimmel had taken the right steps before the attack. The blame, if there was any, rested on the chief of naval operations, Admiral Stark, for not providing all the information his fleet commander needed.

The army board faulted General Short for not preparing his men for a possible attack. It also blamed officials in Washington for not insisting that Short take further actions based on what they knew he was doing to prepare for war. In general, the two new investigations questioned the findings of the Roberts Commission. The new findings seemed to take some of the blame off Kimmel and Short and place it on the top officials in Washington — if not President Roosevelt himself.

## Political Concerns

As the two military branches held their hearings, Roosevelt was seeking a fourth term in office. Although his health was not good, the president was anxious to see the war to its end.

But he faced rumors that still swirled—that he had known of the impending attack on Pearl Harbor before it happened.

In September 1944 journalist John Flynn published a short book called *The Truth about Pearl Harbor*. Flynn was one of the first Pearl Harbor "revisionists"—writers and historians who tried to challenge the government's story about what had happened. Flynn had been an isolationist before the war, helping to found the America First Committee. He also opposed Roosevelt's New Deal and was unhappy with the way it expanded government power. Flynn and some others who disliked Roosevelt wanted to place blame for Pearl Harbor on the president and his closest advisers. Flynn claimed that Roosevelt had been trying to force a war with Japan since January 1941, as a way to get involved in the European war. He also said Roosevelt had ordered Kimmel to keep the ships in dock, which was not true. But Flynn and others managed to raise the issue of whether Americans still really knew the truth about Pearl Harbor.

Most Americans were not thinking about Pearl Harbor or the army and navy hearings as the 1944 presidential election neared. But Roosevelt did not want the hearings to generate any information that might hurt his reelection chances. He discussed the possibility of delaying the end of the army hearings until after the election, but they moved ahead. Secretary of War Henry Stimson persuaded Roosevelt not to tamper with the process.

Roosevelt won his fourth term. But he did not live to see the war's end. On April 12, 1945, he died at his vacation home in Georgia. Harry S Truman, the vice president, then took over the presidency, and the Allies soon finished their wars in Europe and Asia. Against Japan, the Americans used a powerful new weapon, the deadliest ever built: the atomic bomb. One was used on Hiroshima and another on Nagasaki.

Just days after the second bomb fell, Japan agreed to surrender. The island nation wept as the news was broadcast over the radio in the form of a recorded announcement by Emperor Hirohito. It was the first time the emperor had ever spoken to his subjects, now in defeat after the long war in the Pacific. He said that Japan had begun the war "out of our sincere desire to ensure Japan's self-preservation and the stabilization of East Asia." His words hid the reality of the cruelty his soldiers had inflicted on people across large parts of Asia in the name of Japan's "stability." Western scholars also noted that Hirohito never used the word *surrender*, as if he could not admit that Japan had lost a war it had started. What began at Pearl Harbor ended with the total destruction of Japan's cities and the smashing of its imperial ambitions.

But even then, some Japanese soldiers refused to believe that the emperor would surrender, that Japan's quest for empire was over. Captain Mogami Sadao accepted the news when he heard it, but some of the men he commanded didn't. He later said, "They were screaming, 'If Japan accepts [defeat], Japan will perish! Keep fighting resolutely! You must do something!'" Sadao searched out the emperor's brother, Prince Mikasa, who assured him that the emperor knew what he was doing. The war had to end. Faced with the dishonor of defeat, some Japanese officers killed themselves. Others, hiding out in remote caves on Guam and other islands, never heard the war was over and were still prepared to fight on. Some lived in this isolated way for years.

# The Military Hearings

The following excerpts from the final reports of the Navy Court of Inquiry and the Army Pearl Harbor Board provide perspective.

*The Court is of the opinion that Admiral Kimmel's action[s], taken immediately after assuming command . . . were adequate and effective. . . . The Court is of the opinion that Admiral Harold R. Stark, U.S.N., Chief of Naval Operations and responsible for the operations of the Fleet, failed to display the sound judgment expected of him in that he did not transmit to Admiral Kimmel . . . important information which he had regarding the Japanese situation and, especially, in that, on the morning of 7 December, 1941, he did not transmit immediately the fact that a message had been received which appeared to indicate that a break in diplomatic relations was imminent, and that an attack in the Hawaiian area might be expected soon.*

General George C. Marshall failed in his relations with the Hawaiian Department in the following particulars:

*(a) To keep the Commanding General of the Hawaiian Department [General Short] fully advised of the growing tenseness of the Japanese situation which indicated an increasing necessity for better preparation for war, of which information he had an abundance and Short had little.*

*(b) To send additional instructions to the Commanding General of the Hawaiian Department on November 28, 1941, when evidently he failed to realize the import of General Short's reply of November 27th, which indicated clearly that General Short had misunderstood and misconstrued the message of November 27 and had not adequately alerted his command for war.*

The Japanese surrendered on September 2, 1945, aboard the USS *Missouri*.

## Congress Takes Action

By the fall of 1945, President Truman had released the final reports of the army and navy boards, so the country knew that Admiral Kimmel and General Short were not the only ones responsible for the disaster at Pearl Harbor. Truman also suggested that others deserved some blame. "I came to the conclusion that the whole thing is the result of the policy which the country itself pursued. The country was not ready for [war] preparedness. Every time the President made an effort to get a preparedness program through the Congress, it was stifled. Whenever the President made a statement about the necessity of preparedness he was vilified [attacked] for doing it. I think the country is as much to blame as any individual in this final situation that developed in Pearl Harbor."

Since December 7, 1941, eight different investigations had been conducted, including several private ones. Now Congress wanted to study the information gathered in those reports and conduct its own investigation. The Joint Committee on the Investigation of the Pearl Harbor Attack held its first meeting in November 1945. For several months, the lawmakers questioned members of the military and the government. The witnesses ranged from George Elliott, one of the privates who had manned the radar on Oahu before the attack, to George C. Marshall, by then a five-star general, and Henry Stimson, the current secretary of war.

The Joint Committee's hearings lasted several months. The testimony filled thirty-nine volumes, and the final report was more than four hundred pages long. All six Democrats and four Republicans issued a majority report, which came to this major conclusion:

> The ultimate responsibility for the attack and
> its results rests on Japan, an attack that was
> well planned and skillfully executed. . . . The
> committee has found no evidence to support
> the charges, made before and during the
> hearings, that the President, the Secretary of
> State, the Secretary of War, or the Secretary
> of Navy tricked, provoked, incited, cajoled,
> or coerced Japan into attacking this Nation
> in order that a declaration of war might be
> more easily obtained from the Congress.

Two Senate Republicans, Homer Ferguson and Owen Brewster, issued a separate minority report. Ferguson gave several reasons for rejecting the majority report. For one, he didn't think the committee had all the facts about the diplomacy between the United States and Japan before the war. More importantly, he believed the evidence clearly showed that President Roosevelt and his top aides were directly responsible for leaving Pearl Harbor unprepared for the attack. The majority, though, thought the commanders in Hawaii and some officials in Washington had not properly prepared for an attack. People made mistakes, but no one had deliberately left Pearl Harbor open to an attack.

## The Rise of the Revisionists

The report of the Joint Committee did not satisfy the critics of Franklin Roosevelt. The *Chicago Tribune* had opposed Roosevelt's New Deal and had been strongly isolationist before the war. Early in 1947, it welcomed a new book by one of its writers, George Morgenstern. In *Pearl Harbor: The Story of the Secret War*, Morgenstern presented a view common at the *Tribune*: Roosevelt had managed events and withheld facts so he could achieve his goal of bringing America into World War II.

Morgenstern knew his book would stir strong criticism. He was attacking the official story of what happened before Pearl Harbor as told by the Roosevelt administration and its defenders. The reviews, as he expected, were mostly harsh. The *New York Times* reviewer said Morgenstern's aim was to a "reveal a 'monstrous, unbelievable conspiracy' directed by the President against the American people." The critic said of the claim, "to intelligent readers it will

In November 1945 the Joint Committee on the Investigation of the Pearl Harbor attack had its first meeting.

remain unbelievable." But not all intelligent Americans rejected Morgenstern's book. By 1950 a battle of ideas was under way between the revisionists and the historians who accepted Congress's report on Pearl Harbor. The revisionists sometimes referred to their opponents as "court historians." In the past, it was customary for a monarch to have "historians" at the royal court record what happened during his or her reign in a way that would make the ruler look wise, brave, and honorable. The ruler's reputation was understood to be more important than presenting the truth. This was the perspective of the revisionists who believed that the "court historians" wanted to defend Roosevelt no

# Challenging the Majority Report

The minority report issued by Senators Ferguson and Brewster contained the following conclusions.

Minority Report

> The decision of the President, in view of the Constitution, to await the Japanese attack rather than ask for a declaration of war by Congress increased the responsibility of high authorities in Washington to use the utmost care in putting the commanders at Pearl Harbor on a full alert for defensive actions before the Japanese attack on December 7, 1941. . . . High authorities in Washington failed in giving proper weight to the evidence before them respecting Japanese designs and operations which indicated that an attack on Pearl Harbor was highly probable and they failed also to emphasize this probability in messages to the Hawaiian commanders.

Congressman Frank Keefe, a Republican on the committee, signed the majority report but also issued his own statement. Here are some of his views:

*The high civilian and military officials in Washington who had skillfully maneuvered Kimmel and Short into the position of exclusive blame knew at the time all the hidden facts about Pearl Harbor, at least as much and probably more than this investigation has been able to uncover. . . . With full knowledge of Japan's intentions prior to the attack, Washington had one plain duty to the American people. That duty was to inform them of their peril. This was not done. Washington had a further duty to make sure that our forces were ready to meet the attack by furnishing their commanders afield and afloat with all available information, or by evaluating that information and giving them appropriate clear and categoric instructions.*

matter what. The mainstream historians claimed the revisionists distorted the facts to suit their views.

One of the leading revisionists was Harry Elmer Barnes. He promoted perhaps the most extreme view about Roosevelt: that the president deliberately kept information from Kimmel and Short so that their inaction would encourage Japan to launch a war. Then, Barnes claimed, Roosevelt hid these efforts to get the country into war and focused blame on the commanders in Hawaii.

In 1953 Barnes released a collection of essays by various revisionists. One of them was Charles Tansill, who in 1952 wrote a book that presented Roosevelt as having looked for a "back door" to war in Europe. Tansill noted that Hitler had not struck the United States, which would have given Congress a reason to declare war; he proposed, instead, that Roosevelt had "turned to the Far East and increased his pressure upon Japan."

Over the decades, new writers took up the revisionist cause. And even some mainstream historians began to see valid points in some revisionist arguments. Martin Melosi, for one, agreed that Roosevelt and his top advisers did try to cover up what had happened before the attack, though not because they had sought the attack itself. Instead, Melosi argued that the leaders "wished to protect Roosevelt's foreign policy by quashing a political controversy over the question of responsibility." With the nation at war, Roosevelt did not want investigations and debate that would weaken his ability to fight the war or run the government.

Melosi also believed that the revisionists had won a major victory in historiography—the larger view of history, how it is written and what influences historians. In examining

Pearl Harbor, professional historians could not ignore the revisionists and their claims, even if they still rejected most revisionist views.

## Another Round of Battle

Those words appeared in 1983, as Melosi reviewed two recently published books about Pearl Harbor. One of them was soon considered the last word on Pearl Harbor: Gordon Prange's *At Dawn We Slept*. Prange had served as a government historian in Japan after the war and interviewed both U.S. and Japanese officials. Before he died in 1980, Prange had written 3,500 pages of material in which he tried to show the events of Pearl Harbor from both sides. The book published under his name was a short version of Prange's research done by two former students. In their introduction, the historians wrote that Prange "believed that there were no deliberate villains in the Pearl Harbor story." He put some blame on Kimmel and Short, as others had done. He also noted the failures in Washington: for example, failing to send complete MAGIC information to the commanders in the Pacific. But he rejected virtually all the revisionists' claims while defending Roosevelt, and his work won praise for its accuracy.

If Roosevelt both had wanted Japan to strike first and knew that Pearl Harbor was the target, he could have made sure fewer ships were sitting at dock. Thus it would have made more sense, if the president had in fact been using the "back door" to war, to tell Kimmel and Short what was going on. Prange also rejected the idea that the Pearl Harbor attack was the only way war could have erupted. Even without the bombing, Japan and the United States were moving on opposing paths. And there was no guarantee that Germany would declare war on the United States. The Tripartite Pact between Italy, Germany, and Japan called for the countries to help each other only after one was attacked—not if one member attacked a nonbelligerent nation first. Prange's students had the harshest words for Barnes, saying he rejected certain facts or misunderstood others as he tried to make Roosevelt the "villain" of Pearl Harbor. Barnes, they wrote, relied on "unsupported assumptions and assertions."

*At Dawn We Slept* appeared just before publication of a new revisionist look at Pearl Harbor, John Toland's *Infamy*. Toland wrote histories for general readers. His support for the back-door theory seemed to boost the revisionist cause, at least among those inclined to believe the worst of Roosevelt. Toland wrote that Roosevelt had taken a "calculated risk" in allowing the attack and had ordered a cover-up of the facts after December 7, 1941.

Toland's book drew criticism for taking leaps in logic. Martin Melosi, who believed that there were benign reasons for what he saw as a cover-up, said, "The gaps between evidence and the conclusions in *Infamy* are far too wide." Other historians had similar concerns, with Gerald E. Wheeler calling the book "badly flawed and unreliable."

# Eight

# An Enduring Fascination

A conspiracy involves a group of people meeting, planning, and then carrying out some illegal, and often deadly, action. At times Americans have tried to explain certain events in their history as being part of a conspiracy, even without real proof. At other times, various politicians have seen conspiracies in the formulation and execution of the country's economic policies and its foreign relations. The subject of the book George Morgenstern published in 1947 was the conspiracy he believed Franklin Roosevelt had created before and after Pearl Harbor.

To historians of Pearl Harbor, the revisionists took bits and pieces of historical facts and adapted them to fit a theory that they believed from the start to be true. Thus it is because of the revisionists' failure to examine the "back door to war" idea critically that they are properly dismissed as promoters of a conspiracy theory for which evidence is lacking. Recent revisionists, often not professional historians, sometimes claim to have new facts that add to their case. Professional historians usually say the new information is distorted or doesn't really prove what the revisionists claim. And many point out that conspiracies rely on secrecy. Regarding Pearl

# The Final Investigation?

In the years after Congress's hearings, Husband Kimmel fought to clear his name. He always thought he had been unfairly blamed for the country's unpreparedness at the time of the Pearl Harbor attack, and that the government had never given him a chance to prove this in a military court. After Kimmel died, his family continued the struggle. They asked the military to restore his rank, which had been lowered after Pearl Harbor. The Kimmels also asked Congress to order another study of the Pearl Harbor events. Under pressure from the Senate, the Department of Defense agreed to reexamine the roles both Kimmel and General Short played at Pearl Harbor. Short, too, had been demoted after Pearl Harbor, and his family also was seeking to have their relative's rank restored. The next document produced by Congress, the so-called Dorn Report, found that the two Hawaii commanders were "certainly not solely to blame for the disaster at Pearl Harbor but also certainly not entirely innocent of error." The investigators also found no evidence of a government effort to make them scapegoats. On the other hand, there was "no evidence of government actions to deflect criticism" away from the commanders. In 2000 Congress called on the government to restore the rank of each man, but the military has not acted.

Harbor, they wonder: how could the hundreds of people who had firsthand knowledge of the facts have remained silent for so many years?

## Japanese Reactions

Like the Americans, the Japanese discussed Pearl Harbor after the war, though less extensively. The attack on Pearl Harbor had led to the destruction of two major cities, Hiroshima and Nagasaki, a painful turning point in Japanese and world history. But the war had also led to strong postwar ties between the United States and Japan, which helped Japan develop one of the world's largest economies and a democratic system of government.

In 1994 journalist T. R. Reid reported on some opposing views of Pearl Harbor in Japan. Some people believed war with the United States had been inevitable, "and thus the surprise attack on the U.S. fleet was a legitimate act of war. Others here [in Japan] say it was morally wrong for Japan to start a war no matter what the circumstances." Some Japanese writers have suggested that the secrecy and deception Japan used before the war created a perception in the United States that the Japanese are always sneaky. A Japanese paper said, "Long after, the feeling lingers, and even in economic disputes it has a profound impact on Americans' deep distrust of Japan." Today, though, few if any postwar Americans still think about Pearl Harbor when dealing with Japan.

In 2005 the Japanese newspaper *Yomiuri Shimbun* produced the first of a series of articles about the country's wars of the 1930s and 1940s. The paper asked who was to blame for the decisions that led to war with the United States.

The person most responsible, the paper argued, was Prime Minister Hideki Tojo. He approved both attacking the United States and continuing the war when it was clear that Japan could not win. Next was Prime Minister Konoe Fumimaro. Before Pearl Harbor, he too often supported the wishes of the military, even though he tried to prevent war with the United States. Other lesser government officials and military commanders also shared the blame.

Japanese historians have looked at what their leaders said during the time before Pearl Harbor and their explanations for war. Ienaga Saburō, like others, denies that Japan attacked neighboring lands to end European and U.S. influence in Asian colonies. Japan needed oil and other resources as a result of its own action—invading China. The Americans shut off the supply of oil as a response to that military decision. Saburō said, "There was no reason why Japan had to fight a war against America. It was not inevitable."

At times, some Japanese and Americans have speculated about whether Japan would ever apologize for its surprise attack on Pearl Harbor. In 1994 Emperor Akihito, the son of Hirohito, the wartime emperor, considered visiting Pearl Harbor. Some of his subjects opposed the trip because they didn't want it to seem like an unofficial apology. This stance reflected the view that Japan had had a right to attack, since it faced a threat from the United States. Akihito said at the time that he didn't plan to apologize, and he ended up not going to Pearl Harbor. He said, "It is very important to understand historical truths correctly, but because of my position, I must refrain from touching on this kind of subject." The emperor made a second visit to Hawaii in 2009 and once again did not visit Pearl Harbor.

# From the Waters of Pearl Harbor

If Emperor Akihito had gone to Pearl Harbor, a likely stop would have been the USS *Arizona* Memorial (right). Located in the harbor itself, the memorial sits above the remains of the *Arizona*, which lost 1,177 men during the December 7 attack. Of all the ships damaged at Pearl Harbor, it was the only one never pulled from the waters, though the navy was able to recover spare parts and scrap metal. Six of the damaged battleships were repaired and saw action against the Japanese during the war. Many of the smaller naval ships were also repaired and returned to service. During the war, *New York Times* reporter Robert Trumbull wrote a series of articles detailing the incredible efforts made to pull the damaged ships out of the water and prepare them to sail again. The government censors refused to let the stories run, not wanting the Japanese to know about the work. The newspaper finally released the articles in 2006, to mark the sixty-fifth anniversary of the attack.

In 2009 Japanese emperor Akihito and the empress Michiko visited Hawaii and met with Hawaii's governor Linda Lingle. He chose not to visit Pearl Harbor.

## Another Pearl Harbor?

On the morning of September 11, 2001, Americans watched their TV sets with horror as two planes slammed into the Twin Towers of New York's World Trade Center. Soon, reports came of a plane smashing into the nation's military headquarters, the Pentagon; and then came word of another passenger aircraft crashing in a Pennsylvania field. Altogether, almost three thousand people died as a result of the crashes. With the second Twin Towers impact, President George W. Bush and his advisers knew the United States was under attack. What they didn't know for sure was the identity of the enemy, though the suspicion quickly focused on foreign terrorists, and Americans soon learned that the group al Qaeda was responsible for the attack. President Bush then launched a "war on terror," centered in Afghanistan, to weaken al Qaeda and try to prevent future attacks.

Visitors view an American aircraft carrier moored at Pearl Harbor.

In the days that followed, to many Americans who looked back in history to find a parallel, the obvious example was Pearl Harbor. In both cases, the country received a surprise attack that killed thousands of people. But what were the true parallels between 9/11 and Pearl Harbor? What were the differences? With 9/11, was the United States prepared for the possibility of this kind of attack on mostly civilian targets? Were there failures to communicate information that could have lessened the impact of the attack? Was any one government agency to blame, or were the events of 9/11, like that of Pearl Harbor, the result of human error on many levels?

Some people called the 9/11 attacks a criminal act. Was Pearl Harbor? If the two attacks were not similar in nature, was going to war the proper response in both cases? And what were the differences between the nature of the enemy in each attack?

As with Pearl Harbor, the 9/11 attacks led to calls for government investigations. These showed that before

September 11 the government had more information about the terrorists than it had originally admitted. But was the information as detailed as the intelligence President Roosevelt had about Japanese intentions in November and December 1941? And could diplomacy have prevented the 9/11 attack? What relation, if any, did the United States have with the terrorists before September 2001?

As with Pearl Harbor, some Americans once again saw a conspiracy at work. Revisionists appeared claiming that the government could have done more to prevent 9/11. In the more extreme views, some 9/11 revisionists suggested that the Bush administration allowed the attacks to happen, or even helped plan them. The government's goal, the revisionists argued, was to rally support for an already planned invasion of Iraq. Professional historians reject these claims, just as they reject the theories of the Pearl Harbor revisionists.

## Pearl Harbor Today

Today, "Pearl Harbor" brings to mind surprise attacks and the state of being unprepared for a disaster that might have been foreseen. The day that lives in infamy offers examples of governments and militaries divided, international struggles, and historians trying to make sense of it all, examining the facts. Countless writers have made suggestions about what lessons Pearl Harbor offers. They have stressed the need for good intelligence, for a well-equipped military, for honest diplomacy backed by the willingness to use force, if necessary. Some have pointed out that a powerful nation should not ignore the military talents or will of a supposedly weaker one, because a nation ready for war has many tools—especially surprise and deception.

# Timeline

**February 1922**   At the Washington Conference, nine nations, including Japan and the United States, accept limits on the size of their navies.

**February 1923**   The Japanese government approves a secret defense policy for Japan that sees a future war with the United States as likely and states the need for Japan to prepare for it.

**July 1930**   The London Conference angers Japanese military officers, as Japan accepts further limits on the size of its navy.

**September 1931**   Japanese forces launch a military campaign to seize total control of Manchuria, part of north-eastern China.

**November 1932**   Franklin D. Roosevelt is elected president of the United States.

**January 1933**   Adolf Hitler becomes the leader of Germany.

**July 1937**   Japan goes to war with China; the United States offers the Chinese limited aid.

**September 1939**   Germany invades Poland, starting World War II.

**May 1940**   The U.S. fleet is moved from California waters to Pearl Harbor.

**July 1940**    Roosevelt calls for an embargo on certain goods sold to Japan.

**September 1940**    Japan sends troops into northern Indochina and signs a military agreement, the Tripartite Pact, with Germany and Italy.

**November 1940**    U.S. military intelligence breaks the code Japan uses to send messages to its diplomats in Washington, D.C.; Japanese admiral Isoroku Yamamoto has his first ideas for a surprise attack on Pearl Harbor.

**February 1941**    Admiral Husband Kimmel takes command of the U.S. fleet based at Pearl Harbor.

**February 1941**    General Walter Short takes control of the defense of Pearl Harbor.

**July 1941**    Japanese troops move into southern Indochina; the United States responds with an embargo on oil sales to Japan.

**October 1941**    General Hideki Tojo is named prime minister of the Japanese government.

**November 26, 1941**    Secretary of State Cordell Hull delivers what the Japanese see as an ultimatum; a fleet prepared to strike Pearl Harbor leaves Japan.

**November 27, 1941**   At Pearl Harbor, Admiral Kimmel and General Short receive messages warning them of the possibility of war.

**December 1, 1941**   The Japanese government officially approves going to war with the United States.

**December 2, 1941**   Admiral Yamamoto gives the order to carry out the Pearl Harbor attack.

**December 6, 1941**   U.S. intelligence intercepts the first parts of a message to Japanese diplomats, indicating on behalf of the imperial government that war is at hand.

**December 7, 1941**   The final part of the message arrives; Japan begins to attack Pearl Harbor and the Philippines, then officially declares war on the United States.

**December 8, 1941**   Roosevelt asks Congress to declare war on Japan.

**December 9, 1941**   Secretary of the Navy Frank Knox goes to Hawaii, beginning the first investigation of what happened at Pearl Harbor.

**January 1942**   The Roberts Commission issues its report, blaming Kimmel and Short for not preparing for the Japanese attack.

**July 1944**   In separate hearings into what happened at Pearl Harbor, both navy and army investigators conclude that military officials in Washington deserved partial blame for the nation's unpreparedness.

**September 1944**    John Flynn publishes a revisionist look at what happened before Pearl Harbor, blaming Roosevelt for the success of the attack.

**April 12, 1945**    Roosevelt dies and Harry S Truman becomes president.

**August 6, 1945**    The United States drops the first of two atomic bombs on Japan, and the Japanese soon surrender.

**September 2, 1945**    Surrender ceremony takes place in Tokyo Bay aboard the USS *Missouri*; Japan officially surrenders to the United States, ending World War II.

**November 1945**    In Congress, the Joint Committee on the Investigation of the Pearl Harbor Attack holds its first meeting.

**July 1946**    The committee issues its report, which does not blame Roosevelt or his top advisers.

**January 1947**    *Chicago Tribune* reporter George Morgenstern publishes the first major revisionist book about Pearl Harbor.

**1952**    Historian Charles Tansill publishes a book accusing Roosevelt of using Pearl Harbor as a "back door" to war.

**1983** In his book *Infamy*, John Toland suggests that Roosevelt knew about the coming attack on Pearl Harbor and let it happen; Gordon Prange's *At Dawn We Slept* offers a detailed look at what all professional historians accept as the proper view of the events, mainly blaming human error and miscommunication and dismissing the idea of a conspiracy to take the country into World War II by an alleged "back door" of Pearl Harbor.

**1991** The U.S. Navy releases a report showing that its intelligence officers had messages from the Japanese Navy about the Pearl Harbor attack, but the raw reports were not decoded until 1942.

**1995** Another investigation ordered by Congress shows that Admiral Kimmel and General Short were not solely responsible for the inadequacy of the defense of Pearl Harbor, but they share some of the blame.

**2009** Japanese emperor Akihito travels to Hawaii but chooses not to visit Pearl Harbor.

# Notes

## Introduction

p. 6, "All war . . . we are far away": attributed to Sun Tzu. Available at Sun Tzu's Art of War, http://suntzusaid. com/book/1 (accessed on 12 February 2010).

## Chapter One

p. 9, "TO, TO, TO": Japanese radio signal, quoted in Mitsuo Fuchida and Masatake Okumiya, *Midway: The Battle That Doomed Japan, The Japanese Navy's Story*. Annapolis, MD: Naval Institute Press, 2001, p. 51.

p. 9, "TORA, TORA, TORA": Japanese radio signal, quoted in John Toland, *The Rising Sun: The Decline and Fall of the Japanese Empire, 1936–1945*. New York: Modern Library, 2003, p. 212.

p. 10, "the biggest sighting . . . ever seen": Joseph Lockard, quoted in John Costello, *Days of Infamy*. New York: Pocket Books, 1994, p. 230.

p. 10, "Don't worry about it": Lieutenant Kermit Tyler, quoted in Costello, *Days of Infamy*, p. 230.

p. 13, "we believe . . . actively loyal": Report by Curtis Munson, quoted in Greg Robinson, *By Order of the President: FDR and the Internment of Japanese Americans*. Cambridge, MA: Harvard University Press, 2001, p. 76.

p. 14, "This is no test . . . . the Japanese!": Daniel K. Inouye, quoted in David Colbert, ed., *Eyewitness to America*. New York: Pantheon Books, 1997, p. 399.

p. 15, USS *Arizona* Memorial, National Park Service, www. nps.gov/archive/usar/PHcas.html; Michael E. Haskew, *The World War II Desk Reference*. New York: Grand Central Press, 2004, p. 35.

p. 16, "I . . . lay flat . . . . Two hits!": Mitsuo Fuchida, quoted in Fuchida and Okumiya, *Midway*, pp. 53–54.

p. 17, "We were . . . . die at any moment": Louis Mathieson, quoted in Haskew, *The World War II Desk Reference*, p. 34.

p. 18, "each report . . . than the last": Grace Tully, quoted in Colbert, *Eyewitness to America*, p. 404.

p. 18, "the Japanese . . . decision for him": Harry Hopkins, quoted in Robert Dallek, *Franklin D. Roosevelt and American Foreign Policy, 1932–1945*. New York: Oxford University Press, 1979, p. 311.

p. 18, "a date which . . . the empire of Japan": Franklin D. Roosevelt, *Great Speeches*. John Grafton, ed. Mineola, NY: Dover, 1999, p. 114.

## Chapter Two

p. 23, "clash with our Empire . . . against the United States": Imperial National Defense Policy, quoted in Sadao Asada, *From Mahan to Pearl Harbor: The Imperial Japanese Navy and the United States*. Annapolis, MD: Naval Institute Press, 2006, p. 102.

p. 23, "bound hand and foot and thrown into jail": Kato Kanji, quoted in Asada, *From Mahan to Pearl Harbor*, p. 157.

p. 26, "has no territorial ambitions . . . a passing storm": Hirosi Saito, "A Japanese View of the Manchurian Situation," *Annals of the American Academy of Political and Social Science*, Vol. 165 (January 1933), pp. 159–166.

p. 28, "Japan's action . . . existence": Konoe Fumimaro, quoted in Kazuo Yagami, *Konoe Fumimaro and the Failure of Peace in Japan, 1937–1941: A Critical Appraisal of the*

*Three-Time Prime Minister*. Jefferson, NC: McFarland & Company, 2006, p. 27.

## Chapter Three

p. 29, "ordinary Japanese . . . these things as the truth": Ienaga Saburō, quoted in Haruko Taya Cook and Theodore F. Cook, *Japan at War: An Oral History*. New York: New Press, 1992, p. 442.

p. 29, "In recent years . . . the Japanese people": rebel statement, quoted in Toland, *The Rising Sun*, p. 21.

p. 30, "No treasure trove . . . as well": Yosuke Matsuoka, quoted in Toland, *The Rising Sun*, p. 48.

p. 34, "They were sacrificing . . . . in '37 and '38": Kumaguya T. Tokuichi, quoted in Cook and Cook, *Japan at War*, p. 47.

p. 35, "Their [the Japanese] victory . . . . danger of being shot down": F. Tillman Durdin, "Japanese Atrocities Marked Fall of Nanking after Chinese Command Fled," *New York Times*, 9 January, 1938, p. 38.

p. 36, "But . . . remain neutral in thought as well": Franklin D. Roosevelt, radio address, 3 September 1939. *Selected Speeches, Messages, Press Conferences, and Letters*. Basil Rauch, ed. New York: Holt, Rinehart and Winston, 1957, p. 225.

p. 36, "I do not believe . . . . war is insanity": Burton K. Wheeler, radio address, 31 December 1940. Available online at Teaching American History, www.teaching americanhistory.org/library/index.asp?document=1592 (accessed on 3 March 2010).

p. 37, "would wage . . . more and more provocative":

Franklin D. Roosevelt, quoted in Thomas G. Paterson, J. Garry Clifford, and Kenneth J. Hagan, *American Foreign Relations: A History Since 1895*. Boston: Houghton Mifflin, 2000, p. 182.

p. 38, "Don't miss the bus!": quoted in Toland, *The Rising Sun*, p. 60.

p. 38, "when one of the three . . . . Chinese-Japanese conflict": Tripartite Pact, 27 September 1940. Available online at the Avalon Project, http://avalon.law.yale.edu/wwii/triparti.asp (accessed on 10 June 2010).

p. 38, "stand firm . . . man to man": Yosuke Matsuoka, quoted in Toland, *The Rising Sun*, p. 64.

p. 39, "control the western Pacific . . . . Japanese-American relations:" Yosuke Matsuoka, quoted in Gordon W. Prange with Donald M. Goldstein and Katherine V. Dillon, *At Dawn We Slept: The Untold Story of Pearl Harbor*. New York: Penguin Books, 1991, p. 7.

p. 39, "Japan's last step . . . in the Southwest Pacific": Cordell Hull, quoted in James E. Auer, ed. *From Marco Polo Bridge to Pearl Harbor: Who Was Responsible?* Tokyo: *Yomiuri Shimbun*, 2006, p. 107.

p. 41, "We should avoid . . . at all costs": Konoe Fumimaro, quoted in Yagami, *Konoe Fumimaro and the Failure of Peace in Japan, 1937–1941*, p. 128.

p. 42, "In the U.S.–Japanese negotiations . . . . our diplomatic efforts": Konoe Fumimaro, quoted in Yagami, *Konoe Fumimaro and the Failure of Peace in Japan, 1937–1941*, p. 132.

## Chapter Four

p. 44, "could embark . . . than our normal Pacific Coast bases?": James O. Richardson, quoted in Roland H. Worth Jr., *Pearl Harbor: Selected Testimonies, Fully Indexed, from the Congressional Hearings (1945–1946) and Prior Investigations of the Events Leading Up to the Attack*. Jefferson, NC: McFarland & Company, 1993, p. 359.

p. 46, We should do . . . the very first day": Isoroku Yamamoto, quoted in Asada, *From Mahan to Pearl Harbor*, p. 279.

p. 47, "To make victory . . . in the White House": Isoroku Yamamoto, quoted in Prange, *At Dawn We Slept*, p. 11.

p. 48, "Japan, not we, is on the warpath": Joseph Grew, *Ten Years in Japan*. London: Hammond & Hammond, 1945, p. 310.

p. 48, "the fact . . . pass on the information": Joseph Grew, quoted in Worth, *Pearl Harbor: Selected Testimonies*, p. 48.

p. 48, "no move . . . for the foreseeable future": U.S. Naval Intelligence, quoted in Toland, *The Rising Sun*, p. 151.

p. 50, "not impossible . . . not be improbable": Walter C. Short, quoted in Fred Borch and Daniel Martinez, *Kimmel, Short, and Pearl Harbor: The Final Report Revealed*. Annapolis, MD: Naval Institute Press, 2005, p. 54.

p. 50, "I would have been . . . in Hawaiian waters": Walter C. Short, quoted in Gordon Prange, with Donald M. Goldstein and Katherine V. Dillon, *Pearl Harbor: The Verdict of History*. New York: Penguin Books, 1986, p. 343.

p. 51, "they did not expect . . . United States and Japan": Walter C. Short, quoted in Worth, *Pearl Harbor: Selected Testimonies*, p. 256.

p. 51, "without allowing . . . to ourselves": Franklin D. Roosevelt, quoted in Dallek, *Franklin D. Roosevelt and American Foreign Policy*, p. 307.

p. 52, "It is clear . . . as an enemy": diplomatic cable, quoted in Akira Iriye, *Pearl Harbor and the Coming of the Pacific War: A Brief History with Documents and Essays*. Boston: Bedford/St. Martin's, 1999, p. 80.

p. 53, "When Britain and America . . . . demonstrated to the world": Isoroku Yamamoto, quoted in Samuel Eliot Morison, "The Rising Sun in the Pacific," *Foreign Affairs*, Vol. 70, No. 5 (Winter 1991), p. 154.

p. 53, "begin war . . . assure survival": Hideki Tojo, quoted in George Victor, *The Pearl Harbor Myth: Rethinking the Unthinkable*. Washington, D.C.: Potomac Books, 2007, p. 238.

p. 55, "I believe . . . no signs of uneasiness": quoted in Record of Imperial Conference, 1 December 1941, in Iriye, *Pearl Harbor and the Coming of the Pacific War*, pp. 88–95.

## Chapter Five

p. 56, "hostile action . . . aggressive move": quoted in Victor, *The Pearl Harbor Myth*, pp. 82–83.

p. 57, "gave me a jolt": Edwin Layton, quoted in Costello, *Days of Infamy*, p. 154.

p. 58, *"Niitakayama nobore"*: quoted in Auer, *From Marco Polo to Pearl Harbor*, p. 124.

p. 59, "How much damage . . . . has not changed at all": Matome Ugaki, quoted in Prange, *At Dawn We Slept*, p. 349.

p. 61, "I never dreamed . . . attack the harbor": Leon Kolb, quoted in Dana Bartholomew, "'Infamy' Times Two for U.S. Pearl Harbor Survivor," *Daily News*, 7 December 2001. Available online at www.thefreelibrary.com/%2 7INFAMY%27+TIMES+TWO+FOR+U.S.+PEARL +HARBOR+SURVIVOR:+NEVER . . . -a080647955 (accessed 23 March 2010).

p. 64, "keg of dynamite . . . . the South Pacific area": Franklin D. Roosevelt, Letter to Emperor Hirohito, 6 December 1941, *Selected Speeches*, p. 297.

p. 65, "The Japanese will not . . . . too strong": William Pye, quoted in Prange, *At Dawn We Slept*, p. 470.

p. 65, "There was a plane . . . . This is the real thing!'": Ruth Erikson, Oral History of the Pearl Harbor Attack, Naval History and Heritage Command, www.history.navy. mil/faqs/faq66-3b.htm (accessed on 14 June 2010).

p. 65, "They came zooming out . . . part of the sky": Daniel Inouye, quoted in *Eyewitness to America*, p. 399.

p. 66, "At least two Japanese bombers . . . . setting an oil tank afire": Eugene Burns, "Tokyo Declares War on US and Britain after Attack." *Providence Journal*, 7 December 1941, p. 1. Available online at www.stg. brown.edu/projects/WWII_Women/TimeLine/Pearl Harbor.gif (accessed on 15 June 2010).

p. 67, "Japan has done . . . . to fear in this war": "Japanese Premier's Story." *New York Times*, 8 December 1941, p. 5.

p. 69, "I saw ships . . . . Pearl Harbor": Fred Lowrey, University of Hawaii Center for Oral History. Available online at www.oralhistory.hawaii.edu/pages/audio_ pages/warau.html (accessed on 15 June 2010).

p. 69, "This success . . . . how powerful is the Imperial

Navy!": Samadu Sanagi, quoted in Prange, *At Dawn We Slept*, p. 540.

p. 69, "a bad dream . . . not be true": Edwin Layton, quoted in Costello, *Days of Infamy*, p. 233.

## Chapter Six

p. 70, "Execute . . . against Japan": quoted in Toland, *The Rising Sun*, p. 225.

pp. 70, 72, "I was an avid . . . a tremendous shock": Edward Osberg, quoted in *Americans Remember Pearl Harbor*, www.stg.brown.edu/projects/WWII_Women/RA/NCraig/PHMemories.html (accessed on 15 June 2010).

p. 72, "hideous fear that the bombers . . . . we all caught it": Dellie Hahne, quoted in *Americans Remember Pearl Harbor*, www.stg.brown.edu/projects/WWII_Women/RA/NCraig/PHMemories.html (accessed on 15 June 2010).

p. 72, "The people . . . how long it takes": "City Calm and Grim as the War Widens." *New York Times*, 12 December 1941, p. 1.

p. 72, "the desire . . . . in all their history": Carroll D. Alcott, "Why Remember Pearl Harbor?" *Antioch Review*, Vol. 2, No. 1 (Spring 1942), pp. 7–8.

p. 73, "What was supposed to happen . . . before Japan was cleared": Nogi Harumichi, quoted in Cook and Cook, *Japan at War*, p. 55.

p. 73, "I felt as if . . . . everyone was for the war": Itabashi Kōshū, quoted in Cook and Cook, *Japan at War*, pp. 77–78.

p. 73, "It is almost unbelievable . . . be victorious in this war": Fumimaro Konoe, quoted in Yagami, *Konoe Fumimaro and the Failure of Peace in Japan, 1937–1941*, p. 134.

p. 74, "I knew . . . . watching the war go on": Ienaga Saburō, quoted in Cook and Cook, *Japan at War*, p. 442.

p. 75, "We are still pacifists . . . be peacemakers": "Editorial," *Catholic Worker*, quoted in Patricia McNeal, "Catholic Conscientious Objection during World War II," *The Catholic Historical Review*, Vol. 61, No. 2 (April 1975), pp. 226–227.

p. 77, "Because most prewar . . . . had poor eyesight": John Grove, quoted in *Americans Remember Pearl Harbor*, www.stg.brown.edu/projects/WWII_Women/RA/NCraig/PHMemories.html (accessed on 15 June 2010).

p. 77, "I do not believe . . . way they do things": Leland Ford, quoted in Robinson, *By Order of the President*, p. 92.

p. 79, "I don't remember . . . . in working order": Jeanne Wakatsuki Houston, quoted in Lawson Fusao Inada, ed, *Only What We Could Carry: The Japanese American Internment Experience*, pp. 104–105.

p. 80, "diabolic savagery . . . . so-called great powers": "'Diabolic Savagery,' Tokio Calls Coast Evacuation of Japanese," *San Francisco News*, 5 March 1941. Available online at the Virtual Museum of the City of San Francisco, www.sfmuseum.org/hist8/tokio.html (accessed 15 June 2010).

p. 81, "A citizen who . . . . spy or a saboteur": William O. Douglas, *Ex Parte Mitsuye Endo*, 323 U.S. 283 (1944). Available online at http://caselaw.lp.findlaw.com/cgi-bin/getcase.pl?court=us&vol=323&invol=283 (accessed on 15 June 2010).

p. 82, "war president . . . . the confidence of the American people": David Walsh, quoted in C. P. Trussell, "Senate Is Bitter in Hawaii Debate." *New York Times*, 12 December 1941, p. 10.

p. 83, "failed properly . . . . the success of the attack": Roberts Commission Report, p. 19, Available online at www.ibiblio.org/pha/pha/roberts/roberts.html#19 (accessed 1 April 2010).

## Chapter Seven

p. 84, "the demands . . . magnificent courage and understanding": Franklin D. Roosevelt, Annual Message to Congress, 11 January 1944. *Selected Speeches*, p. 340.

p. 87, "out of our . . . stabilization of East Asia": Emperor Hirohito, radio address of 14 August 1945. Available online at www.mtholyoke.edu/acad/intrel/hirohito.htm (accessed on 5 April 2010).

p. 87, "They were screaming . . . . do something!'": Mogami Sadao, quoted in Cook and Cook, *Japan at War*, p. 455.

p. 88, "The Court is . . . . might be expected soon." Report of the Navy Court of Inquiry. Available online at WWII Archives Foundation, http://wwiiarchives.net/servlet/doc/Phnavyreport (accessed on 2 April 2010).

p. 89, "General George C. Marshall . . . . alerted his command for war": Report of the Army Pearl Harbor Board. Available online at www.ibiblio.org/pha/pha/army/chap_6.html (accessed on 2 April 2010).

pp., 90–91, "I came to the conclusion . . . . in Pearl Harbor": Harry Truman, quoted in U.S. Congress Joint Committee on Pearl Harbor Attack. Available online at www.ibiblio.org/pha/pha/congress/keefe.html (accessed on 5 April 2010).

p. 91, "The ultimate responsibility . . . . obtained from Congress": U.S. Congress Joint Committee on Pearl Harbor Attack. Available online at www.ibiblio.org/pha/pha/congress/part_5.html#251a (accessed on 6 April 2010).

p. 92, "reveal . . . against the American people": George Morgenstern, quoted in Gordon A. Craig, "Mythology for the Critics of F.D.R." *New York Times*, 9 February 1947, Book Review, p. 6. With additional comment by Craig.

p. 92, "to intelligent readers it will remain unbelievable": Craig, "Mythology for the Critics of F.D.R."

p. 94, "The decision of the President . . . . Hawaiian commanders": Minority Report, U.S. Congress Joint Committee on Pearl Harbor Attack. Available online at www.ibiblio.org/pha/pha/congress/minority.html#503 (accessed on 6 April 2010).

p. 95, "The high civilian . . . . clear and categoric instructions": Frank Keefe, "Additional Views of Mr. Keefe," U.S. Congress Joint Committee on Pearl Harbor Attack. Available online at www.ibiblio.org/pha/pha/congress/keefe.html (accessed on 5 April 2010).

p. 96, "turned to the Far East . . . upon Japan": Charles Callan Tansill, *The Back Door to War: The Roosevelt Foreign Policy 1933–1941*. Reprint. Westport, CT: Greenwood Press, 1975, p. 616. [Originally published in 1952.]

p. 96, "wished to protect . . . the question of responsibility": Martin V. Melosi, "The Triumph of Revisionism: The

Pearl Harbor Controversy, 1941–1982." *The Public Historian*, Vol. 5, No. 2 (Spring 1983), p. 90.

p. 97, "believed that . . . in the Pearl Harbor story": Prange, *At Dawn We Slept*, p. ix.

p. 98, "villain . . . unsupported assumptions and assertions": Prange, *At Dawn We Slept*, p. 850.

p. 98, "calculated risk": John Toland, *Infamy: Pearl Harbor and Its Aftermath*. Garden City, NY: Doubleday & Company, 1982, p. 318.

p. 98, "The gaps . . . are far too wide": Melosi, "The Triumph of Revisionism," p. 101.

p. 98, "badly flawed and unreliable": Gerald E. Wheeler, *Infamy: Pearl Harbor and Its Aftermath*. Review in *The Pacific Historical Review*, Vol. 53, No. 2 (May 1984), p. 261.

## Chapter Eight

p. 101, "certainly not solely to blame . . . innocent of error": Dorn Report, quoted in Borch and Martinez, *Kimmel, Short, and Pearl Harbor*, p. 90.

p. 101, "no evidence . . . to deflect criticism": Dorn Report, quoted in Borch and Martinez, *Kimmel, Short, and Pearl Harbor*, p. 89.

p. 102, "and thus the surprise attack . . . no matter what the circumstances": T. R. Reid, "Apology, But Not to U.S.—Japan Tells Its People It Fumbled Message before Pearl Harbor." *Washington Post*, 22 November 1994. Available online at http://community.seattletimes. nwsource.com/archive/?date=19941122&slug=1943318 (accessed on 12 April 2010).

p. 102, "Long after . . . deep distrust of Japan": *Asahi Shim-bun*, quoted in Reid, "Apology, But Not to U.S."

p. 103, "There was no reason. . . . was not inevitable": quoted in Cook and Cook, *Japan at War*, p. 445.

p. 106, "It is very important . . . this kind of subject": "Akihito Holds Back on Pearl Harbor Apology." *The Independent*, 4 June 1994. Available online at www.independent.co.uk/news/world/akihito-holds-back-on-pearl-harbor-apology-1420335.html (accessed on 12 April 2010).

# Further Information

## Books

Davenport, John. *The Attack on Pearl Harbor: The United States Enters World War II*. New York: Chelsea House, 2009.

Elish, Dan. *Franklin Delano Roosevelt*. New York: Marshall Cavendish Benchmark, 2009.

Gorman, Jacqueline Laks. *Pearl Harbor: A Primary Source History*. Pleasantville, NY: Gareth Stevens Publishing, 2009.

Phillips, Charles. *Japan*. Washington, DC: National Geographic, 2007.

Stein, R. Conrad. *World War II in the Pacific: From Pearl Harbor to Nagasaki*. Berkeley Heights, NJ: Enslow Publishers, 2011.

## DVDs

*Conspiracy? FDR and Pearl Harbor*. A & E Television Networks, 2008.

*Pearl Harbor: Waking the Sleeping Giant*. Mill Creek Entertainment, 2009.

*The Presidents: FDR*. PBS Home Video, 2008.

*War in the Pacific: From Pearl Harbor to Hiroshima*. Columbia River Entertainment Group, 2008.

## Websites

**The Imperial Japanese Navy**

www.combinedfleet.com/

Created by historians, both professional and amateur, this site offers great detail on all aspects of Japan's navy during World War II.

**Pearl Harbor Attack 1941**

http://history.sandiego.edu/gen/WW2Timeline/Prelude23.html

A detailed timeline of the diplomacy, code breaking, and military events that occurred before the attack. The site also includes a map of the harbor and photos from the battle.

### The Perilous Fight
www.pbs.org/perilousfight/
A companion site to the Public Broadcasting System series of the same name, *The Perilous Fight* features color pictures and videos of World War II. The section on Pearl Harbor includes excerpts from a journal written by a sailor who experienced the attack.

### Remembering Pearl Harbor
http://plasma.nationalgeographic.com/pearlharbor/index.html
The National Geographic Society offers a website with a multimedia, interactive map showing the different phases of the battle. It also has information on the ships and planes both countries used during the attack.

### Remembering Pearl Harbor — The USS *Arizona* Memorial
www.nps.gov/history/nr/twhp/wwwlps/lessons/18arizona/18 arizona.htm.
This site from the National Park Service looks at both the Pearl Harbor attack and the turning of the wreck of the *Arizona* into a memorial site. It features charts, maps, and photos.

### Report of the Joint Committee on the Investigation of the Pearl Harbor Attack, July 20, 1946
www.ibiblio.org/pha/pha/invest.html
This site contains the complete report of the Joint Committee as well as reports from the eight inquiries that came before it.

# Bibliography

## Books

*Annals of America*. Vol. 15. Chicago: Encyclopedia Britannica, 1968.

Asada, Sadao. *From Mahan to Pearl Harbor: The Imperial Japanese Navy and the United States*. Annapolis, MD: Naval Institute Press, 2006.

Auer, James E., ed. *From Marco Polo Bridge to Pearl Harbor: Who Was Responsible?* Tokyo: Yomiuri Shimbun, 2006.

Borch, Fred, and Daniel Martinez. *Kimmel, Short, and Pearl Harbor: The Final Report Revealed*. Annapolis, MD: Naval Institute Press, 2005.

Brendon, Piers. *The Dark Valley: A Panorama of the 1930s*. New York: Alfred A. Knopf, 2000.

Colbert, David, ed., *Eyewitness to America*. New York: Pantheon Books, 1997.

Cook, Haruko Taya, and Theodore F. Cook, *Japan at War: An Oral History*. New York, New Press, 1992.

Costello, John. *Days of Infamy*. New York: Pocket Books, 1994.

Craddock, John. *First Shot: The Untold Story of the Minisubs That Attacked Pearl Harbor*. New York: McGraw-Hill, 2006.

Dallek, Robert. *Franklin D. Roosevelt and American Foreign Policy, 1932–1945*. New York: Oxford University Press, 1979.

Daniels, Roger. *Coming to America: A History of Immigration and Ethnicity in American Life*. New York: Perennial, 2002.

Davis, Kenneth S. *FDR: The New Deal Years, 1933–1937*. New York: Random House, 1986.

Frank, Richard B. *Downfall: The End of the Imperial Japanese Empire*. New York: Penguin Books, 1999.

Fuchida, Mitsuo, and Masatake Okumiya. *Midway: The Battle*

*That Doomed Japan, The Japanese Navy's Story*. Annapolis, MD: Naval Institute Press, 2001.

Grew, Joseph. *Ten Years in Japan*. London: Hammond & Hammond, 1945, p. 310. Available online at http://books.google.com.

Haskew, Michael E. *The World War II Desk Reference*. New York: Grand Central Press, 2004.

Inada, Lawson Fusao, ed. *Only What We Could Carry: The Japanese American Internment Experience*. Berkeley: HeyDay Books, 2000.

Iriye, Akira. *Pearl Harbor and the Coming of the Pacific War: A Brief History with Documents and Essays*. Boston: Bedford/St. Martin's, 1999.

Love, Robert W. Jr., ed. *Pearl Harbor Revisited*. New York: St. Martin's Press, 1994.

McCullough, David. *Truman*. New York: Simon & Schuster, 1992.

Paterson, Thomas G., J. Garry Clifford, and Kenneth J. Hagan, *American Foreign Relations: A History*. Vols. I and II. Boston: Houghton Mifflin, 2000.

Prange, Gordon W. with Donald M. Goldstein and Katherine V. Dillon. *At Dawn We Slept: The Untold Story of Pearl Harbor*. New York: Penguin Books, 1991.

———. *Pearl Harbor: The Verdict of History*. New York: Penguin Books, 1986.

Robinson, Greg. *By Order of the President: FDR and the Internment of Japanese Americans*. Cambridge, MA: Harvard University Press, 2001.

Roosevelt, Franklin D. *Great Speeches*. John Grafton, ed. Mineola, NY: Dover, 1999.

———. *Selected Speeches, Messages, Press Conferences, and Letters*. Basil Rauch, ed. New York: Holt, Rinehart and Winston, 1957.

Spector, Ronald H. *Eagle against the Sun: The American War with Japan*. New York: Free Press, 1985.

Stinnett, Robert B. *Day of Deceit: The Truth about FDR and Pearl Harbor*. New York: Free Press, 2000.

Tansill, Charles Callan. *The Back Door to War: The Roosevelt Foreign Policy 1933–1941*. Reprint. Westport, CT: Greenwood Press, 1975. [Originally published, 1952.]

Toland, John. *Infamy: Pearl Harbor and Its Aftermath*. Garden City, NY: Doubleday & Company, 1982.

———. *The Rising Sun: The Decline and Fall of the Japanese Empire, 1936–1945*. New York: Modern Library, 2003.

Victor, George. *The Pearl Harbor Myth: Rethinking the Unthinkable*. Washington, DC: Potomac Books, 2007.

Wheal, Elizabeth-Anne, et al. *Encyclopedia of the Second World War*. Edison, NJ: Castle Books, 1989.

Willmott, H. P., Robin Cross, and Charles Messenger. *World War II*. New York: DK. 2004.

Worth, Roland H. Jr. *Pearl Harbor: Selected Testimonies, Fully Indexed, from the Congressional Hearings (1945–1946) and Prior Investigations of the Events Leading Up to the Attack*. Jefferson, NC: McFarland & Company, 1993.

Yagami, Kazuo. *Konoe Fuminaro and the Failure of Peace in Japan, 1937–1941: A Critical Appraisal of the Three-Time Prime Minister*. Jefferson, NC: McFarland & Company, 2006.

# Websites

"Akihito Holds Back on Pearl Harbor Apology." *The Independent*, 4 June 1994. Available online at www.independent.co.uk/news/world/akihito-holds-back-on-pearl-harbor-apology-1420335.html.

The American Presidency Project, www.presidency.ucsb.edu.

Americans Remember Pearl Harbor, http://www.stg.brown.edu/projects/WWII_Women/RA/NCraig/PHMemories.html.

Bartholomew, Dana. "'Infamy' Times Two for U.S. Pearl Harbor Survivor." *Daily News*, 7 December 2001. Available online at www.thefreelibrary.com/%27INFAMY%27+TIMES+TWO+FOR+U.S.+PEARL+HARBOR+SURVIVOR:+NEVER...-a080647955.

Bernstein, Richard. "Did We Know We Knew?" *New York Times*, December 15, 1999. Available online at www.nytimes.com/1999/12/15/books/books-of-the-times-on-dec-7-did-we-know-we-knew.html?pagewanted=1.

Burns, Eugene. "Tokyo Declares War on US and Britain after Attack." *Providence Journal*, 7 December 1941, p. 1. Available online at www.stg.brown.edu/projects/WWII_Women/Time-Line/PearlHarbor.gif.

Chamberlain, John. "Pearl Harbor." *Life*, September 24, 1945, pp. 110-120. Available at Google Books, http://books.google.com/books?id=3EkEAAAAMBAJ&pg=PA110&lpg=PA110&dq=marshall+scrambler+phone+pearl+harbor&source=bl&ots=H_X6gGTaCN&sig=pQfPb3Egbjbs24MRudM-ZizqZCA&hl=en&ei=E8iwS5bbG8H88Aa03Ii2BA&sa=X&oi=book_result&ct=result&resnum=1&ved=0CBkQ6AEwADgK#v=onepage&q=marshall%20scrambler%20phone%20pearl%20harbor&f=false.

Conn, Stetson, Rose C. Engelman, and Byron Fairchild. *Guarding the United States and Its Outposts*. Center of Military History, United States Army. Available on line at www.history.army. mil/books/wwii/Guard-US/.

"'Diabolic Savagery,' Tokio Calls Coast Evacuation of Japanese," *San Francisco News*, 5 March 1941. Available online at the Virtual Museum of the City of San Francisco, www.sfmuseum. org/hist8/tokio.html.

*Ex Parte Mitsuye Endo*, 323 U.S. 282 (1944), http://caselaw.lp.findlaw. com/cgi-bin/getcase.pl?court=us &vol=323&invol=283.

"Flashbacks: Pearl Harbor in Retrospective." *Atlantic Monthly*, 25 May 2001. Available online at www.theatlantic.com/past/ docs/unbound/flashbks/pearlharbor.htm.

Flynn, John T. *The Final Secret of Pearl Harbor*. Available online at www.antiwar.com/news/?articleid=4122.

Frazier, Kendrick. "The Pearl Harbor 'Winds Message' Controversy: A New Critical Evaluation." *Skeptical Inquirer*, Vol. 33.2 (March/April 2009). Available online at www.csicop.org/si/ show/pearl_harbor_winds_message/.

Greenberg, David. "Exonerating FDR." History News Network, June 17, 2001. Available online at http://hnn.us/articles/107. html.

Hanyok, Robert J. "How the Japanese Did It." *Naval History Magazine*, Vol. 23, No. 6 (December 2009). Available online at www.usni.org/magazines/navalhistory/story.asp?STORY_ ID=2081.

Hatch, David A. "ENIGMA and PURPLE: How the Allies Broke German and Japanese Codes during the War." Available

online at http://74.125.47.132/search?q=cache:LKFwJaYXOs
YJ:www.usna.edu/Users/math/wdj/papers/cryptoday/hatch_
purple.ps+magic+purple+japan&cd=25&hl=en&ct=clnk&gl
=us.

Martin, James J. "Pearl Harbor: Antecedents, Background and Consequences." *The Memory Hole*. Available online at http://tmh.floonet.net/articles/pearl.html.

Maugh, Thomas H., II. "Pearl Harbor Mini-Submarine Mystery Solved?" *Los Angeles Times*, 7 December 2009. Available online at http://articles.latimes.com/2009/dec/07/science/la-sci-mini sub7-2009dec07.

Milestones, 1937–1945: Diplomacy and the Road to Another War. U.S. Department of State, Office of the Historian. Available online at http://history.state.gov/milestones/1937-1945.

Oral History of the Pearl Harbor Attack. Naval Heritage and History Command. Available online at www.history.navy.mil/faqs/faq66-3b.htm.

Parker, Frederick D. *Pearl Harbor Revisited: United States Navy Communications Intelligence 1924–1941*. United States Cryptologic History, United States Navy. Available online at www.history.navy.mil/books/comint/index.html.

The Pearl Harbor Archive: The Independent Institute. Available online at www.independent.org/issues/article.asp?id=1431.

Pearl Harbor Review – Pearl Harbor. National Security Agency Available online at www.nsa.gov/about/cryptologic_heritage/center_crypt_history/pearl_harbor_review/pearl_harbor.shtml.

Possony, Stefan T., Jerry E. Pournelle, and Francis X. Kane. "Surprise." The Strategy of Technology. Available online at www.pournelle.org/sot/sot_5.htm.

Reid, T. R. "Apology, But Not to U.S.—Japan Tells Its People It Fumbled Message Before Pearl Harbor." *Washington Post*, 22 November 1994. Available online at http://community. seattletimes.nwsource.com/archive/?date=19941122&slug =1943318.

Remembering Pearl Harbor—The USS *Arizona* Memorial. National Park Service. Available online at www.nps.gov/history/nr/twhp/wwwlps/lessons/18arizona/18arizona.htm.

Report of the Joint Committee on the Investigation of the Pearl Harbor Attack, 20 July 1946. Available online at www.ibiblio. org/pha/pha/invest.html.

Report of the Navy Court of Inquiry. WWII Archives Foundation. Available online at http://wwiiarchives.net/servlet/doc/ Phnavy report.

Tetsuya, Takahashi, "Philosophy as Activism in Neo-Liberal, Neo-Nationalist Japan." *Asia-Pacific Journal*, Japan Focus. Available online at www.japanfocus.org/-Takahashi-Tetsuya/2566.

Tripartite Pact. Avalon Project. Available online at http://avalon. law.yale.edu/wwii/triparti.asp.

Trumbull, Robert."Two Years of Hard Work." *New York Times*, 7 December 2006. Available online at www.nytimes.com/2006/ 12/07/opinion/07trumbull.html?_r=2.

University of Hawaii Center for Oral History. Available online at www.oralhistory.hawaii.edu/pages/audio_pages/warau.html.

Wheeler, Burton. Radio address, 30 December 1940. Teaching American History.org. Available online at www.teaching americanhistory.org/library/index.asp?document=1592.

Yamaguchi, Kari. "Documents Shed New Light on Japan's Attack." *Daily Gazette*, 6 December 2001. Available online at

<br>Google News Archives, http://news.google.com/newspapers?
nid=1957&dat=20011206&id=5eEqAAAAIBAJ&sjid=WIgF
AAAAIBAJ&pg=1319,1372946.

## Newspaper and Journal Articles

Alcott, Carroll D. "Why Remember Pearl Harbor?" *Antioch Review*,
Vol. 2, No. 1 (Spring 1942), pp. 6–26.

Borch, Fred L. "Comparing Pearl Harbor and '9/11' Intelligence:
Intelligence Failure? American Unpreparedness? Military
Responsibility?" *Journal of Military History*, Vol. 67, No. 3 (July
2003), pp. 845–860.

"City Calm and Grim as the War Widens." *New York Times*, December 12, 1941, pp. 1, 21.

Craig, Gordon A. "Mythology for the Critics of F.D.R." *New York
Times*, 9 February 1947, Book Review, p. 6.

Doenecke, Justus D. *Day of Deceit: The Truth about FDR and Pearl
Harbor*. Review. *Journal of American History*, Vol. 69, No. 1
(June 2002), pp. 281–282.

Durdin, F. Tillman. "Japanese Atrocities Marked Fall of Nanking
after Chinese Command Fled," *New York Times*, 9 January
1938, p. 38.

Henning, Arthur Sears. "Asserts Pearl Harbor Report Is Incom-
plete." *Chicago Daily Tribune*, 22 July 1946, p. 1.

"How America Was Led to War." *Chicago Daily Tribune*, 21 January 1947, p. 12.

McNeal, Patricia. "Catholic Conscientious Objection during
World War II." *The Catholic Historical Review*, Vol. 61, No. 2
(April 1975), pp. 222–242.

Melosi, Martin V. "The Triumph of Revisionism: The Pearl Harbor Controversy, 1941–1982." *Public Historian*, Vol. 5, No. 2 (Spring 1983), pp. 87–103.

Morgenstern, George. "Author of 'Pearl Harbor' Anticipates the Critics." *Chicago Daily Tribune*, 5 January 1947, p. G6.

Morison, Samuel Eliot "The Rising Sun in the Pacific." *Foreign Affairs*, Vol. 70, No. 5 (Winter 1991), pp. 153–155.

"The Pearl Harbor Report." *New York Times*, 21 July 1946, p. E8.

Saito, Hirosi. "A Japanese View of the Manchurian Situation," Annals of the American Academy of Political and Social Science, Vol. 165 (January 1933), pp. 159–166.

Trussell, C.P. "Senate Is Bitter in Hawaii Debate." *New York Times*, 12 December 1941, p. 10.

"U.S. 'White Paper'; President in Message Reveals How Tokyo Hid Treacherous Aims." *New York Times*, 16 December 1941, p. 1.

Wheeler, Gerald E. *Infamy: Pearl Harbor and Its Aftermath*. Review. *Pacific Historical Review*, Vol. 53, No. 2 (May 1984), pp. 260–262.

White, William S. "Knox Report Puts Disaster Blame on Short, Kimmel." *New York Times*, 6 January 1946, pp. 1, 4.

Zwick, Mark, and Louise Zwick. "Dorothy Day, Prophet of Pacifism for the Catholic Church," *Houston Catholic Worker*, www.cjd.org/paper/pacifism.html.

# Index

Page numbers in **boldface** are illustrations.

# About the Author

MICHAEL BURGAN is the author of more than 250 books for children and young adults, both fiction and nonfiction. For Marshall Cavendish's Perspective On series, he has written *Hiroshima: Birth of the Nuclear Age* and *The Scopes Trial: Faith, Science, and American Education*. A graduate of the University of Connecticut, Burgan is also a produced playwright. He lives in Connecticut.

SSH
BOOK FOR LOAN

WITHDRAWN from The Free Library of Philadelphia
Book contains theft-detection device that may set off alarm.

2011  18
1 acture 2018